The Catapult Loading System: How to Teach 100-Pound Hitters to Consistently Drive the Ball 300-Feet

THE CATAPULT LOADING SYSTEM: HOW TO TEACH 100-POUND HITTERS TO CONSISTENTLY DRIVE THE BALL 300-FEET

How to Teach 100-Pound Hitters to Consistently Drive the Ball 300-Feet

Joey Myers

Fresno

PLEASE REVIEW ON AMAZON

Thank you for downloading my book, please review on Amazon so we can make future versions even better.

CONTENTS

WHAT PEOPLE ARE SAYING...?

*"My son is 12 and I have used some of the teaching the Hitting Performance Lab are posting on here and **my son hit the ball over 280 feet several times already in the game not just practices and also hit the fence on the fly on 300 feet field**, so what this guy is teaching works, a least for my son...He weighs about 110 now, but what I have noticed is how consistent his power has become thank you so much for your help, I played 10 years of professional baseball and I wish I could of used some of this advice."*
  – Sandy Arecena (via email)

---

*"Hey bud...Jayden had his best batting practice ever last night. **Hit at least 9 balls around 300-feet or farther**. I'm so happy with his progress so far. You are truly an amazing coach and I appreciate everything you have done for Jayden. I know he still has a long ways to go and he will keep working with you to get there. Thanks again brotha."*
  – Sal Mandel (via text message, 12yo son is about 115-lbs)

---

*"Want to give a big thanks to Joey Myers – Hitting Performance Lab. I've read a few of your books, great stuff. My son changed his swing in the off season. **Now he leads batting average, homeruns, rbi's**. By the way, we played in a wooden bat tournament. One of two kids to homer with a wood bat. Thanks again."*
  – Joe Harris (via Facebook)

---

*"I changed my 10yr old to this style midway through the season. He was batting .320 no HRs! **Last 30 games he batted .560 as a righty and .584 as a lefty with 5 HRs!** He plays major ball! The difference it made with him was fun to watch!!!"*
  – Jack A. Martin (via Facebook)

---

*"I've been incorporating some of your thoughts into my sons routine. He's 5'1 and about 110lbs. **He's gone from hitting his first HR over 4 weeks ago to 6 in the last two tournament weekends.** I'm talking absolute seeds and not just floaters. He's moved from the bottom of the lineup to batting second on one of the best 12u teams in the state of Georgia. Thanks for helping out guys like me."*
  – Brent Rouse (via email)

---

*"Hey Joey, first, thanks for the course on hitting. My 12 year old has always been a solid hitter but after working the PPD stuff **he has started hitting the ball over the fence on the big field at 315 ft to center**. It has taken a few months work but well worth it, as he is seeing the results of the work and his teammates and coaches on his new*

travel team are amazed at the bombs flying out there. He's 5'3 and 120 pounds. I think the key has been getting low and turning the numbers and releasing. He always had trouble with the low strike, and he's stoked to now be on plane for that one as well now."

  – Greg Del Mar (via email)

_____

"Just want to say thank you. My son who is 14, 5'6" and maybe 120lbs is really benefiting from your drills. We modified his batting swing during this past off-season, per your instructions, and have definitely seen the power go up. He is a lefty that used to hit a lot of singles to opposite field. Now **we are seeing doubles, triples, and 2 HR's so far early in our season...to right field**. *He was never a pull hitter, but now is able to go that way with power while still going to left with a pitch. Thanks!"*

  – Greg Uehling (via email)

_____

"My 70-pound 11 year old hit one over 200 fence today. *Joey studies what the best do and uses research to back it up. If you don't agree with him that's fine, teach to swing down and through and read Charlie Lau like I did as a kid. My 75lb son is learning to hit in the air and can hit 3x his body-weight in distance."*

– Brandon Lewis (via Twitter & Facebook)

_____

"I ordered the book and read it in 1 afternoon. My son is 8 years old and weights 65 pounds. He has always been a great contract hitter but little to no power. I have worked with him on his grip and finger pressure, and his load and hiding his hands and **he hit three off the fence which is 175 feet where we play**. *That is a big improvement from just being able to get the ball over the infielders to driving it off the fence. Great book, easy read."*

– Mathew Payne (via Facebook)

_____

"I just got done with a practice where **two 65 lb 7 and 8 yr olds can hit over 150 ft**. *Bat speed baby."*

– Matt Gardner (via Facebook)

_____

"Finished the book a few weeks ago. **Ideas are backed by Zepp measurement. Real numbers no smoke and mirrors**. *Started applying to practices for my 7 and 10 year old. Already see more consistent ball flight and increase in bat speed. Thanks Joey"*

– Guillermo Garcia (via Facebook)

_____

"Hey coach, even with Mia still hitting with her hands near hear head, **Mia in a 3 game span, hit 3 home runs over the fence and a stand up double, three singles and four walks**. *Only made one out, a shot down first. She never had a series of games like this an especially playing with girls that are this much older. Mia is able to play in 12 and under, but she is playing in the high school division. Our sights are getting ready for October 4 and 5. That is when we go to the U of Florida camp. Their assistant coach has called Mia's coach twice in the past week and wants us to call him this week. Let keep on course and work hard, thanks so much for all your help coach."*

  – Primo Buffano (via email)

"You're the first I've seen to successfully articulate and adopt human movement into anything practical. What you've put together is very impressive. Most of what I've come across, even from those in the profession that understand human movement are assessment methods and tools to analyze movement and posture only to sell a few methods to correct dysfunction issues. Few are willing or able to explain human movement the way you have. These principles are the key for both performance and injury management. I appreciate the time and effort you put in to help those looking to perfect their craft and for those of us out their trying to help them."
– H. Orlando James

"Love your stuff. Your system turned a unsure, very-bottom-of-the-order 12U baseball player into a #3-in-the-order-all-season confident 13U hitter..."
– Bruce Bergen (via email)

*"Your new videos are awesome. Your product is becoming **one of the best on the internet for sure!**"*
– Andy Rando (via email)

*"I first bought Jaime Cevallos book last spring that led me to Baseball Rebellion then to you. Your presentation style is great. My older son clicked with the 2 parts to the swing rather than all the pieces of the puzzle drills. My other son is two years younger and **saw powerful results in just a few drills.**"*
– Corey Mir (via email)

"F$% you are really informed Joey...I'd say you are better at being a swing coach now than you ever were as a hitter.....meaning you were top notch then but **now you are at hall of fame level stuff!!**"*
– Rob Suelflohn (via email)

*"I'm 59 years old and still play slow pitch league and tournament ball. I have occasional power and am not a big guy at 5'9 and 180 lbs. It's always driven me crazy when I'd drive the ball deep once in awhile only. I've spent 5 years working on a tee and doing internet research, but really there has not been much improvement. Then I took the course. Yesterday in batting practice, **I was destroying the ball to all fields 90% of the time. The guys were gasping as the ball left my bat with a sick sound.** The corrections I have made to my swing using your course are FINALLY allowing me to be the hitter I knew that I could be! Thanks Joey."*
– Russ Lederman (via email)

*"Big fan of the catapult system. Colin is killing it! As you have pointed out it naturally stops arm barring additional benefit for Colin it has helped with his timing allowing the ball to travel deeper. **2 Grand Slams this past weekend in Cooperstown NY tournament.**"*

– Chad Casamento (via email)

"Great job Joey! I have been replaying so many swings during this year's playoffs. After watching your videos and buying the truth videos i am all in. You can replay any of Ortiz's swings and they all are the same right now. He is a man amongst boys this postseason. **What you are teaching is so abundant in MLB but not amongst the youngsters and most coaches.** *Keep up the good work man!"*

– Fred Holdsworth (via email)

"13 year pro ball player here. I just wanted to say how much i enjoy your videos/emails and I couldn't agree more with the mechanics and techniques that you teach. There is so many concepts to hitting out there that are being taught, yet i feel like **you're on the right track to unlocking what it takes physically & mechanically to translate what the best in the world are doing every day.** *Unfortunately for me the science has come too late in my career as i approach the light at the end of my "tunnel". Keep up the great work."*

– YouTube Username: TGARCIA247

"It may take some time but the rest of the world will eventually come around to understanding *that with hitting the simple movements we are trying to explore and teach are the best. I love the fact that Hitting Performance Lab uses great MLB hitters, past and present, to prove that these ideas will work, are working, and have always worked. Keep it up Joey, you have me completely converted. The proof is in the hitters we work with. Many of mine are starting achieve exit velocities that they never thought possible. Averages are up, power is up. I have three girls who will be playing D1, 6 playing D2, 2 going to Juco's this next fall and one younger girl attending several D1 camps this month. Thanks to you for doing the science and providing convincing evidence. Keep up all the good work."*

– Ronny Weber (via email)

"The first time I read your book the catapult system, I have to admit, I was a little underwhelmed. I thought there was a lot of fluff for just a couple principles. There was a few nuggets there that made me think I should give it another try. I saw some of your videos on your website and I started to kinda get a few more nuggets. I tried what I thought a few of your principles with my son and I was unimpressed because I think I didn't get it and kinda started thinking I got ripped off by your book. **I think it was partially because I was being closed minded and partially the information was a bit over my head as I'm a fan of baseball but not a student of the game.** *(I believe I am becoming a student)*

*So I started listening to other hitting gurus, some of which echo parts of your system (**unfortunately not the whole, they are getting there**) and I started watching videos of some of these MLB guys who kind of embodied your system and I started picking up on things.*

Well, I picked up your book about on the "Ugly Truth About Hitting Ground Balls". Let me say, I should have started with that book. It may be a small book but its awesome, has a lot more information than I expected and so simple and easy to understand. Plus, it made a lot of sense. (truth always does)

So I decided to reread the Catapult System book again, highlighting points as I went along. **It as if the skies opened up to me, I understood what you were trying to tell me before and it all makes sense.** *It just started to* *click for me. The book, coupled with your videos, helped me properly communicate your principles, which I didn't understand before but I understood now, to my son who was confused the first time I tried it out when I didn't fully understand, now understands what I am talking about and the results so far after definitely in the right direction.*

*I'm introducing these principles little by little but he is getting it and it is beautiful! He is a big boy for his age, a power hitter for his team but he started to slump during the Dixie Youth World Series (prior to me implementing your principles) yesterday was our first real practice where **I started implementing a few of these principles and the results were line drives in the deep outfield** and we are not done yet! I am confident and optimistic about his swing the more we work at adding your method to his swing. Please forgive my ignorance and close mindedness. Thank you so much for this information and your continued discoveries. I was blind but now I see!"*
– Tony Ford (via Facebook DM)

———————

Following video of one of my local hitters Orin H., who at the time was **11yo and 98-pounds, hitting a 300-foot double**. We had been working together for 2.5 years up to this point. Here's the text message from his dad, who played 4-years of college baseball at Chico State:

"This is Orin hitting the farthest ball he's ever hit. It landed a couple feet short of the warning track in Manteca, which is right around 300-feet away"

http://gohpl.com/orinh300footshot

The following two videos are of the same hitter, Temo, at **13yo and 115-pounds hitting the ball 300-feet**. He's now **14yo weighing 135-pounds consistently hitting 360-foot shots**. I have only been working with him and his younger brother a short while, but Coach Mark Palacios had been working with him for over 2 years, teaching him the same system I teach:

- **Video #1:** http://gohpl.com/temo300footshot1
- **Video #2:** http://gohpl.com/temo300footshot2

ACKNOWLEDGEMENTS

First and foremost I have to **thank my most loving and supportive wife and family**. I spent many of nights on a deadline, to get this book done, alone in our bedroom hacking away at the keyboard.

Tiffany Myers, who **I'm lucky to have snagged before some other hairy-backed-knuckle-dragger**, and with over 9 years of marriage, you complete me.

This is also for my 4 year old son Noah, and 9 month old daughter Gracen. You guys will learn the value of hard work on whatever passionate curiosity you find yourself in. Mommy and Daddy will help keep providing oxygen to that fire making it as big as you want it.

I want to thank Rann Dasco for the beautiful front and back cover design. You did a fantastic job girlie! **You made me feel like I had BIG shoes to fill with the content.**

I need to also thank Jonathan Rosen for helping me edit this book. To find an editor who edits for a living and coaches youth baseball, is a unique alignment for such specialized information.

And to the over 20,000+ coaches, instructors, and parents out there that tune into my blog on a weekly basis and send comments, questions, critiques, and testimonials…**I couldn't do this without you guys and gals**. You're the fuel that keeps me going. Hearing how this stuff is affecting your young hitters never gets old, and PLEASE, like I always say…keep me updated!

Lastly, **a BIG THANK YOU to my local and online lessons**…I couldn't ask for better students who not only get it done on the field, but in the classroom as well. I haven't met a hitter yet, male or female, that doesn't work as hard in the classroom as they do on the field. I'm proud of you all, keep up the good work.

INTRODUCTION

"In times of change, learners inherit the earth, while the learned find themselves beautifully equipped to deal with a world that no longer exists."
– Eric Hoffe

Fixed Versus Growth Mindset Coaching

When it comes building consistently powerful hitters, this book will provide you with the pathway to get there.

However, I think the most important aspect to **bridging the gap between what the coach teaches and what the player absorbs** has to do with Mindset...

Coaches can be split up into two groups.

1. Fixed Mindset
2. Growth Mindset.

According to Dr. Carol Dweck, in her bestselling book *Mindset: The New Psychology of Success*,

"In a fixed mindset, people believe their basic qualities, like their intelligence or talent, are simply fixed traits. ***They spend their time documenting their intelligence or talent instead of developing them****. They also believe that talent alone creates success—without effort."*

Here are some things you hear **FIXED Mindset** coaches saying,

- You can't teach a Little Leaguer to hit like a Major Leaguer because they aren't strong enough.
- Hand speed can't be coached.
- Natural hitters are just born.
- Hitting is subjective and is different for everybody.
- The greatest hitters just have great hand-eye coordination.
- That 12u 100-pound hitter can consistently hit the ball 300-feet because they're hitting with a HOT bat.
- He/She can hit the ball hard and far because of their body mass.

All of those are to the contrary of Dr. Dweck's definition of a Growth Mindset coach:

"In a growth mindset, ***people believe that their most basic abilities can be developed through dedication and hard work****. Brains and talent are just the starting point. This view creates a love of learning and a resilience that is essential for great accomplishment."*

These coaches find a way. They ask the right questions. They ask, "Why not?" They don't rest on elite-level playing or decades of coaching experience.

The objective of a **Growth Mindset** coach is to learn principles first, or "rules". Then, design methods to stay within those lines, not the other way around. You'll learn more about this in CHAPTER 1.

I'll let Billy Murray give Growth Mindset coaches a word of caution in dealing with Fixed Mindset coaches on social media:

"It's hard to win an argument with a smart person, but it's damn near impossible to win an argument with a stupid person."

Why?

From Henry Ford:

"If you think you can do a thing or think you can't do a thing, then you're right."

One puts the forest before the trees (versus missing the forest for the trees), and the other is swatting a piñata with one eye blindfolded!

I get it, we all want to be heard and validated as being knowledgeable in a subject, but **high credibility in the wrong place is highly misleading**.

Some go to extreme lengths to *IMMEDIATELY* make their presence known. Here are some Fixed Mindset saying tip-offs:

- "I've played [X-number] years professionally and I should know."
- "I've been coaching for 30+ years, and this is why you should listen to me."
- "I've studied millions of hours of video analysis of only the best hitters. I know what I'm talking about"
- "I've put a lot of work into the cages, and that's how I know what I'm talking about"

Don't get me wrong, the last two points above have their place and CAN be effective in learning and seeing success patterns, BUT **massive effort going in the wrong direction can be gross negligence**.

Besides, it takes A LOT of effort in the cages and hours of video analysis to stumble onto the right answers. But, I have a more elegant solution that will dramatically cut your learning time in half!

You'll know what to look for, so you can SUPERCHARGE your time in the cages and also for when you're doing video analysis. You'll read about this in CHAPTER 2.

Willful ignorance.

I heard this term on Facebook and love it! People online defend their hitting philosophy and theories to the death, even if human-movement principles validated by science, reveal the opposite.

I mentally play the "What if...Strip" game with Fixed Mindset coaches...

WHAT IF this person NEVER...

- Played in the Big Leagues...
- Coached for 30+ years...
- Studied millions of hours of video...
- Put a lot of work into the cages...

...IF we stripped them of their primary credibility indicator, THEN I ask:

- What do they actually know?
- Who or what have they studied? (Physics, Bio-Mechanical, Psychology, Exercise Science sources? Not baseball or softball)
- What kind of consistent or inconsistent results do they get with their hitters?

We'll get deeper into the Credibility Fallacy in CHAPTER 3.

Fixed Mindset coaches are stuck. They regurgitate the same information they've been taught in the past without question. They may even say their hitting philosophy is a science, but it's not. It's a pseudo-science. Their **copy and duct-taped together hitting philosophy reeks of uncertainty**. We'll get more into that in CHAPTER 4.

Here's one of my favorite quotes by Dan Farnsworth:

"Doing a thing and understanding a thing do not automatically qualify you to teach a thing."

And it's so true!

I can tell with 100% confidence that I have not:

- Played Professional baseball,
- Coached for over 30 years,
- Studied millions of hours of only the best hitters on video, or
- Put in as much work in the cages as others say they do...

So, why listen to me?

Because of:

- What I actually know,
- Who and what I've studied, and
- The results my hitters are getting.

We'll drill deeper into these points in the following CHAPTERS, but what I think is VERY IMPORTANT for those who never played ball past Little League or 12u softball,

...That **you too, can be a hitting expert**.

All you need is a passionate curiosity to learn and apply the human-movement principles that are validated by science, to hitting a softball or baseball. I'm going to teach you how to conduct fool-proof swing experiments, **so that you can use your findings to show people who won't take you seriously**.

You'll learn my swing-experiment-blueprint in CHAPTER 4.

And I'm going to break it down for you, so don't worry if you didn't do well in science class back in school.

CHAPTER 5 will take you through the science of springy fascia and spinal-engine-mechanics. This is the WHY behind the methods we discuss in the later chapters. You can skip this one, but please return to it later, so you have ammunition for Fixed Mindset coaches who won't believe the results your hitters are getting.

CHAPTERS 6 through 11 will take you through the practical methods and drills my hitters are using to **consistently triple, or at least double, their body-weight in batted ball distance**.

Lastly, CHAPTER 12 will walk you through, how to train these newly-learned hitting techniques. I believe the training is as important, if not more critical, than the mechanics you'll be learning in this book.

I had a third-year pro-hitter drive up from San Diego (about a 7-hour drive for me, one-way), comment that he thought the training by itself was worth the trip! And he spent a fortune in time and money to work through a whole weekend with me.

What You'll Learn

Here's what you're going to learn in the upcoming pages:

- Why hitting philosophy fails and principles that are validated by science succeed.
- **Why you shouldn't make video analysis FIRST-priority, when modeling elite hitters.**

- What 30+ year coaching experience and pro players won't tell you, and how the information source you focus on can dramatically cut down your learning curve.
- How to **become a hitting expert when you've never played higher than Little League**.
- There's a BIG advantage to learning how the body actually loads (and it's not what you're thinking).
- A simple method that helped Babe Ruth to consistently crush the ball with some of the heaviest bats ever used.
- Elite-hitters revealing ways to hit balls with High-Exit-Speeds, swing after swing, using three elements even a 4-year-old can understand.
- At last, the secret to transitioning grooved batting practice swings into game at-bats is revealed.

WHY is this Important to you now?

There are four reasons…

Most "hitting stuff" we've learned is DEAD WRONG. It's based off philosophy and theory, and with the technology available today, we can test the value of those hitting philosophies.

Nowadays, everyone is a hitting "expert". How do we differentiate between an effective versus an ineffective approach? This is important because it's not how PRO someone is, how many years of coaching they've accumulated, how many man-hours of video analysis they've done, or even how many hours of lessons they do in a given day. You can't argue with science and powerfully consistent results.

"Confusion" between mechanical causation equaling correlation. Can you put backspin on a ball by swinging down on it (i.e. negative barrel Attack Angle)? Yes, you can. But, will the hitter consistently get the ball in the air that way? No. In this case, swinging down does not consistently put the ball in the air with authority, and IS NOT what the best are REALLY doing on slow motion video.

Big difference between what's "real" and what's "feel". When Mike Trout says he works at 'getting on top of the ball', that doesn't mean Johnny's coach should go out and share with his team this method. In fact, Mike Trout says this to himself to protect his swing from HIS natural tendency to upper cut too much, like he says to 'chicken wing'. The cues that MLB and professional hitters use are often lost in translation with the younger-end user.

Is the Information in this Book for you?

First, we WILL NOT be talking about:

- 'Squishing bugs',
- 'Swinging down on the ball', OR
- 'Loading & exploding the hips'.

Second, this is specifically about **how to apply human movement 'rules' to hitting a moving ball**, and not about hitting 'philosophies' or 'theories' that DO NOT predictably work in LIVE case studies.

Third, the information in this book is based on the success my personal hitters have had both online and locally, plus **the hundreds of coaches, who've duplicated the results, if not bettered them by using this system**.

The House Rules

Here's what I'm not promising...

    1. No "get powerful hits, quick".
    2. No "do nothing, and crush the ball".
    3. **My results aren't remotely typical.**
    4. Most people who buy ANY "consistent-power-swing" training, will not have success with getting consistent power in their hitters.

Addressing point numbers one and two above...

Some of my 12-years-old and under hitters, weighing around 100-pounds, don't start consistently driving the ball 300-feet right away. Some take 2.5 years to get to consistency, whereas before they do it "every once in awhile". Other hitters, although rare, achieve this in less than 6-months. This seems to be the range for the hitters I work with.

It depends on work ethic and what David Epstein calls 'learn-ability', in his book, *The Sports Gene: Inside the Science of Extraordinary Athletic Performance.*

Addressing point numbers three and four above...

I encourage my hitters to work hard on the things we go over, and to keep on trying even after hitting major obstacles.

Most young hitters don't do that. They just show up for a lesson or gather information and "get ready" to work...or they throw in the towel and quit at the first bump in the road.

It took a lot of hard work for my hitters to start seeing favorable hitting outcomes.

Interestingly, it was the work with my hitters that gave me the inspiration to write this book.

The bottom line is, I have no idea what your results may or may not be.

And it's not my place to try to predict that. **Your success is up to you, as always.**

Onward...

1

CHAPTER 1

"As to methods, there may be a million and then some, but principles are few. ***The man who grasps principles, can successfully select his own methods.*** *The man who tries methods, ignoring principles, is sure to have trouble."*
– Ralph Waldo Emerson

Principles OVER Methods

Principle, not to be confused with a school "principal" (a spelling mistake, which by the way, I have embarrassingly made in the past), is defined by Google:

"A fundamental truth or proposition that serves as the foundation for a system of belief or behavior or for a chain of reasoning."

The Hitting Performance Lab objective is **applying human-movement-principles, or "rules", that are validated by science, to hitting a baseball or softball**.

This includes both Newtonian and non-Newtonian principles. And both of these will become clearer to you in the following pages.

The human-movement "rules" contained in this book however, ARE NOT the same as "pseudo-science", or as well-known Physicist, Dr. Richard Feynman refers to it, as 'Cargo-Cult-Science'. This too, will be addressed in the following pages.

Think of hitting principles as bumpers in the gutters of a bowling alley. The path the bowling ball takes down the lane DOES NOT matter, just as long as it is confined between the bumpers.

Some may refer to principles as hitting "absolutes". However, their definition is built on many hours of seeing patterns in video analysis, not in the human-movement-principles we'll be discussing in this book.

Mark my words,

Hitting instruction will shift toward principle based programming in the next 5 years, but for now, a majority of coaches and instructors are missing the forest for the trees. Instructors using the coaching cues:

- 'Squishing the bug',

- 'Loading and exploding the hips',
- 'Loose muscles are quick muscles', and
- 'Hitting starts from the ground up'...

...are **oblivious to the fundamental rules of human-movement that effectively allow a hitter** to consistently triple their body weight in batted-ball-distance.

In other words,

I have a growing group of 10-14-year-old hitters weighing around 100-lbs, who're consistently hitting the ball over 300-feet.

That's the length of a football field!!

And let me reassure those fast-pitch softball coaches, these principles work for the young ladies as well. **Since the girls are hitting a bigger, heavier ball, they may not see a tripling of their body-weight in batted-ball-distance, but at least a doubling.**

So, for a 100-pound young lady, that's at least 200-feet with a proper launch angle. Not bad, I'd say.

What's more...?

Movement Principles are found in Other Explosive-Rotational-Athletes

Look,

These human-movement-principles work for ALL explosive-rotational-athletes.

In other words, **baseball or softball hitters don't play by different rules, like some FIXED Mindset hitting instructors might say**.

Let me explain...

Rob Suelflohn, who was a top-5 U.S. Shot-Putter in the mid 1980's (he consistently launched a 16-lb, iron cannon ball over 70-feet), invested in my, *The Truth About Explosive Rotational Power* online video course a few years ago, **to help him compete in Masters Shot-Put competitions**. These competitions are for those Track & Field athletes over the age of 30.

Alexandra Franco, a teacher from Portugal, invested in the same, *The Truth,* course **to help her own tennis game, but more importantly, to better the tennis athletes she coaches.** Specifically, she wanted to learn more about what Physicist and Electrical Engineer, Dr. Serge Gracovetsky refers to as, The Spinal Engine. You'll learn more about this in CHAPTER 5.

I've also had quite a few golfers contact me to discuss the same human-movement-principles to better their golf game.

Part of the criteria I use to know whether we're talking a principle or a theory...

...Whether we're talking male or female, young or more seasoned, black or white, **human-movement-principles are present in ALL explosive-rotational-athletes**.

Coaches ask me if the principles in this book only work with baseball players.

Nope.

Fast-pitch and slow-pitch players are humans too! lol

When I stumbled onto Thomas Myers's book, *Anatomy Trains*, Myers gave examples of Javelin and Discus-Throwers, and pitchers using the same principles. We have no immediate relation by the way.

I then went onto study Shot-Putters, Hammer-Throwers, Olympic Divers, and Lacrosse Throwers...and to my surprise...I was seeing the same things, albeit packaged slightly different.

What was clear?

That even though the bowling ball sped forward using a slightly different path, it stayed between the lane bumpers nonetheless.

A Shot Putter is looking to throw a 12-16-pound iron ball as far away from their body as possible. They don't have to hit an object coming at them, so the Shot-Put athlete can afford to NOT look in the direction he or she is launching their object.

A hitter, on the other hand, must track the object they're looking to hit as far and as hard as they can, in a direction that's away from the body. So, how a hitter uses the body's tension and compression forces may not look as extreme, but it's still **tapping into the same elastic-energy-storage-system as the Shot-Putter**. We'll cover springy fascia more in depth in CHAPTER 5.

Check out the following, ESPN's *Sports Science* video of Major League Lacrosse athlete, Paul Rabil, who registered the fastest ML Lacrosse throw of 111-mph:

http://gohpl.com/prlacrosse

Watch at about the 1:50 video mark, and **note the position Paul Rabil puts his body in before he slings the lacrosse ball**. This is The Catapult Loading System showing up in a Major League Lacrosse player.

You'll see an eerily similar approach with the following best athletes competing in:

- Shot-Put
- Javelin, Hammer, and the Discus-Throw
- Tennis
- Golf
- Pitchers

The good news for you coaches is…

It's not just me getting the hitters, I'm hands-on with, consistent results, but **other coaches using *The Catapult Loading System* are getting the same, if not better, outcomes with their hitters!**

Rules of the Game (the THREE O's)

Generally speaking, there's a three-step process for using these principles, to get hitters consistently tripling their bodyweight in batted ball distance…

1. **Objective** – know what result you want your hitters to get,
2. **Obey** – keep the bowling ball rolling between the "bumpers", and
3. **Order** – proper sequencing of movements.

Know what result you want your hitters to get

This typically comes in the form of what consistent negative results are your hitters getting right now?

Too many ground-balls…too many fly-balls…dominating one side of the field…striking out too much…not barreling the ball consistently…or a total lack of power?

Once we know where we want to reverse course, then we look to…

Keep the bowling ball rolling between the "bumpers"

This is where we look to the Newtonian and non-Newtonian "rules" of human movement to guide our path.

Examples of **Newtonian Laws of Physics**:

- Gravitational Reaction Forces

- Conservation of Linear Momentum
- Conservation of Angular Momentum
- Centripetal v. Centrifugal Forces
- Transfer of Energy

Examples of **Non-Newtonian Laws**:

- Springy forces of Fascia
- Spinal engine mechanics
- Bio-Mechanics in a general sense
- Strength and Conditioning systems

Once we know where we want to go and the bowling "bumpers" we're going to stay between, then we want to follow the...

Proper sequencing of movements

This is VERY important. Some may refer to this as the proper sequencing of the kinetic chain.

However, **a vast majority don't understand where the kinetic chain sequence starts and ends**. Many would argue, "from the ground up", but I disagree. And I will address this in CHAPTER 5.

In the old days, if you were one number off, while dialing a friend's phone number, you would reach the WRONG person.

If a hitter does one step out of sequence (or leaves it out completely), then they will not, with certainty, hit the ball with consistent power.

Here's an illustration of my point...

When my wife and I bought our first house in 2010, for years I battled keeping a lush green lawn. Stupidly, I didn't seek out a mentor until I got tired of seeing it yellowing, spotty, and weed ridden.

A friend of mine, I found out, was really good at growing green lawns. He did it for a living, so I asked for his advice...

What do the steps or sequence look like to building a lush green lawn? This is assuming you haven't drenched the ground in weed killer beforehand...

1. Give the remaining grass/weeds a buzz cut.
2. Generously cover the ground in grass seed appropriate for that time of season, preferably in moderate climate, fall (rye) or spring (bermuda/fescue),
3. Keep the ground moist,
4. After about 3 weeks, put on a granule grass fertilizer, weed-killer combo,
5. Keep the ground moist.
6. The more sun you get, the faster the grass will grow, and
7. At about week-6, you should have quite a bit of green lush grass.
8. And at this time, it's okay to cut it.

This is the proper sequence of events to grow a green, lush lawn. Before this knowledge, I realized I was leaving out one or more of these steps, and wasn't reaping the rewards.

When it comes to hitting, **you have to follow the proper sequencing of movements to get the results** we'll be analyzing in this book.

Otherwise, you're running east looking for a sunset.

Does Causation Equal Correlation?

If I wear a green shirt, and coincidently on the same day, it rains…

Does that mean that I can make it rain by wearing a green shirt?

Of course not.

In this case, **the cause of rain doesn't directly correlate with wearing a green shirt**.

In the hitting world, does swinging down on the ball (negative barrel attack angle) create backspin and power?

Most will say yes!

Yes, swinging down can create backspin.

But here's my question…

What's your objective? Consistent power?

The cause of consistent power isn't because of swinging down.

Quite the contrary,

Instead of getting the ball in the air, it will give you more consistent ground-balls.

Don't believe me?

Go out to an open field, have someone throw to you behind an L-screen, and take 200 cuts while chopping down on the ball.

Record on a sheet of paper how many ground-balls, line-drives, and fly-balls you hit.

My hallucination will be that you'll have a majority of ground-balls, which is, if you're truly chopping down on the ball.

A home-run is where a specific Ball-Exit-Speed (speed of batted ball off the bat), barrel launch or attack angle (positive), spin rate, and hang time meet.

Backspin is great but only a part of the causation-correlation equation; in other words, it's not the direct cause of consistent power. Swinging or chopping down on the ball WILL most certainly NOT give your hitters consistent power.

One other thing I wanted to address, because there will be Fixed Mindset coaches reading this book that default to the following hitting cue…

"Hit the Ball on the Ground!"

Is this sound advice?

I wrote a HUGE rant on this titled: *"The UGLY Truth About Hitting Ground Balls"*, at the following url: http://gohpl.com/gbssuck

This post accumulated over 4,200+ Likes on Facebook.

I'm not going into every point I make in that post here, but I do want to cover one biggie…

Taylor Gardner, co-creator of the Backspin Tee, brought this to my attention and I was like "Duh!"

What's one of the golden rules most pitchers across the nation are taught?

Keep the ball down in the strike zone.

WHY?

So the hitter hits the ball on the ground.

What part of the ball are pitchers wanting the hitter to hit?

The top!

Hitting coaches, when your default strategy is to "hit the ball on the ground", **you're affirming the game plan of WHAT PITCHERS WANT HITTERS DOING!!!**

In other words, *you're leading lambs to the slaughter!*

Of course, there are rare instances when we want hitters putting the ball on the ground, like Hit & Runs, and possible move-the-runner over scenarios.

But, hitting the ball on the ground MUST NOT be a default strategy.

Let me offer up a word of CAUTION to those coaching younger hitters (12u on down).

I don't care if the fielders can't play catch at that age.

What happens if you run across a team that can play catch, and the only thing your hitters know how to do is chop down on the ball, breaking off a lot of worm burners?

Let me give you a clue...

YOU WILL LOSE.

And most likely, this will happen when the stakes are high, like in tourney championship play, where you'll be facing better defenses.

...Maybe not at 8u because most young squads do not know how to play catch yet, but you'll start seeing the writing on the wall in two years. **The losing will start small, then by 12u, you will find it hard for your troops to win a game.**

So, what's the answer?

Line drives, duh!

Even deep down, I think pro ground-ball coaches think line drives are the answer.

Then how come they don't teach their hitters to hit them?

Lack of knowledge? Fixed Mindset? Willful Ignorance?

My guess is, **they don't understand how to get their hitters consistently elevating the ball with AUTHORITY**.

Ground-balls are easier outcomes to cue because all you do is tell a hitter to:

- 'Swing down on the ball',
- 'Get on top of the ball',
- 'Swing down the mountain', or
- 'Chop down on the ball'...

And BAM!!

Out comes a consistent ground-ball.

The same can be said of a Fly-ball, but most of these coaches think a ground-ball is better than a fly-ball.

Is it?

I disagree.

Take a look at this data snapshot from FanGraphs.com about MLB hitters in 2014:

they're just different.

Let's take a look at a little bit of data to get started. Here are the results on each type of ball in play from 2014:

Type	AVG	ISO	wOBA
GB	.239	.020	.220
LD	.685	.190	.684
FB	.207	.378	.335

First, let's define some acronyms because I know some of you may not be too versed in Sabermetrics:

- GB = Ground-ball
- LD = Line Drive
- FB = Fly-ball
- AVG = Batting Average
- ISO = Isolated Slugging Percentage
- wOBA = Weighted On-Base Average

You may be familiar with the first four, but maybe not the last two...

Basically, **Isolated Slugging Percentage is a measure of raw power**. It's similar to Slugging Percentage, but doesn't include singles in the calculation. So, doubles, triples, and homers are being counted, and then being divided by a hitter's at-bats.

According to FanGraphs.com, Weighted On-Base Average is,

"Weighted On-Base Average combines all the different aspects of hitting into one metric, weighting each of them in proportion to their actual run value. While batting average, on-base percentage, and slugging percentage fall short in accuracy and scope, **wOBA measures and captures offensive value more accurately and comprehensively."**

Now that we've defined terms...

I think most of us coaches can agree that Line Drives are the hitter's main objective. Can I get an Amen on that?

But the question is, what's better for hitters (or worse for pitchers), a ground-ball or fly-ball?

Well, looking at the graph above:

- **32-point DECREASE in Batting Average** with Fly-balls over Ground-balls,
- **358-point INCREASE in ISO** with Fly-balls over Ground-balls...AND
- **115-point INCREASE in weighted On-Base Average** with Fly-Balls over Ground-balls.

Two out of three for Fly-balls over Ground-balls isn't half bad – it'll get you in the Hall of Fame!

No seriously, **what's the golden rule to winning games?**

Score more runs than the other team.

I'd give up 32-points in Batting Average to gain 358-points in raw power, AND a 115-point increase in run-producing value ANY DAY.

Hitting the ball on the ground as a default strategy is clearly inferior to elevating the ball with authority especially at the High School level on up...

2

CHAPTER 2

"Whenever you find yourself on the side of the majority, it is time to pause and reflect."
– Mark Twain

Video Analysis MUST Come Second To Principles

How do you know what you're looking at, if you don't know what you're looking for?

Most video analysis zealots, who know better, look for swing patterns consistently seen in elite hitters. And may refer to them as hitting "absolutes".

And for the most part, I agree with these.

One clear example that most Growth Mindset coaches understand, would be that elite hitters DO NOT 'squish the bug' with their back foot. We can clearly see their back foot un-weight, or body-weight momentarily shift off their back leg.

The hitting instructors that hold video-analysis as priority one, know a high-level swing when they see one. Heck, they've looked at so many!

Most likely, they're well versed on most hitting philosophies and theories out there.

They've **borrowed, cut, and duck-taped together their own unique hitting philosophy**.

And most I've talked to, get pretty good results with their hitters using this method.

It sounds like a solid process to learn what makes up an effective swing, right?

What's more? *(and here's what I think is the drawback...)*

This has taken these hitting instructors 10-15 years of wading through muck and separating wheat from the chaff. What works is kept, and what doesn't is discarded.

Do I have a problem with this method of learning?

Not necessarily.

But, I do have a problem with how long this process takes for someone without the slightest clue.

Spending hours and hours, every day pouring over slow-motion video footage, looking for answers, DOES NOT appeal to me one bit. **I'm as obsessed as the next person when it comes to hitting**, but I do have a family that I actually want to spend time with!

Where does a new coach start then?

And don't get me wrong, I use slow-motion analysis in my business to observe and prescribe solutions for hitters.

However, I'm offering up a more elegant solution.

Let's dramatically reduce the learning curve...

Learn the "rules" of human movement FIRST

Remember the Ralph Waldo Emerson quote from earlier...?

*"The man who grasps principles can successfully select his own methods. **The man who tries methods, ignoring principles, is sure to have trouble.**"*

The question we should be asking is, how does the human body actually load for explosive rotational power?

And let me give you a clue, it has nothing to do with a hitter "walking their hands away from the body".

So what does the latest and greatest research say on the topic of explosive rotational power?

Most hitting experts will say the body is like a series of rubber bands that stretch and fire.

They aren't totally wrong, because in a nutshell, this is how muscles behave.

But what they don't know of, or refuse to learn, is **the presence of a springy, connective tissue that ties the movement of muscles, bones, and joints together**.

A springy *glue* if you will.

This springy glue is what small sluggers seem to use more effectively than big ones...and the benefits are two-fold:

- **Makes repeatable power achievable for any size, age, and gender hitter**, AND
- Allows the body to move through more naturally safe spinal positions.

In CHAPTER 6, we'll get into more depth with this science of repeatable power, but for now, I want to get the point across that we MUST look at principles first, then at video-analysis second.

Because many big hitters that are commonly studied like Albert Pujols, Mark McGwire, and Bryce Harper can be misleading to analyze.

Wa??

Here's a cautionary tale I want you to remember...

Bigger hitters can be successful despite ineffective mechanics, not because of them.

A smaller hitter, like Dustin Pedroia, cannot get away with ineffective mechanics, at least not with any hopes of competing for over 11-years in the Big Leagues like he has.

Consider the following Hitting Performance Lab case study coming from Martin White, whose son, Hudson, came in second-place in the 2016 14u/15u home-run derby power contest, which was held at the Texas Rangers ballpark in Arlington...

Hudson "The Hawk" White came in second-place, **breaking the contest record for hitting 11 consecutive home runs, which averaged 395-feet**.

What's my point?

This is the same contest, Blaze Jordan hit two monster shots over 500-feet.

14 year old Hudson White is 5-foot, 7-inches, 135-pounds…and Blaze Jordan is 6-foot, 2-inches, 217-pounds…Hudson beat Blaze in the derby!

Marty, Hudson's dad, has been teaching the principles found at my website, and the same ones found in the book you're currently reading, for the past couple of years to his son – who, as you can see – tripled his bodyweight in batted ball distance during the contest.

Hudson White at the 2016 14/15u homerun power challenge at the Texas Rangers Ballpark in Arlington. Photo courtesy: Martin White (dad)

And if you think a metal minus-5 bat was to blame for Hudson's performance, then there are **witnesses who've documented that he's hit balls over 395-feet with Hickory** (that's wood by the way). 'Nuff said?

Someone on Facebook asked me to analyze Blaze Jordan's swing…

Why would I do that?!!

I replied back, WHY don't you want to see me analyze Hudson's swing?

Because he's doing MORE with LESS!!

Now, **you can't hit two 500-foot bombs at 14u without doing something right**. Hot bat or not. And from the looks of Blaze's swing, he seems to embody what we talk about in this book.

But my point is, coaches MUST have strict criteria for swing-modeling, and not use what "big bodies" like Blaze Jordan has, to teach from.

Again, how do you know what you're looking at, if you don't know what you're looking for?

Here's what Hudson's dad Marty had to say about the teaching principles taught in this book:

*"Hello, I just wanted you to know that I have followed you for years and teach your principles to my 14u son who just came in second place at the 15u power showcase in Arlington Texas ahead of the world champion Blaze Jordan . He also **broke the world record for most consecutive home-runs in a row at 11**. He was a year younger and 50-100lbs smaller than all the other contestants who were made up of the best hitters in the country. It was the most amazing thing that anyone had ever seen. I wanted to share the video with you and hopefully you can help make it go viral. All the hype is about Blaze Jordan for hitting a 503 ft home run, but for a smaller younger kid to go out and break the world record for most consecutive and beat blaze in the final round to come in 2nd place is a major feat. My son is a leadoff hitter. So **all hit hits were 395ft line drives**. This is your student. This is the result of your teachings. I am very grateful!"*

Please CLICK to watch Hudson White's 11-consecutive-homer round in the contest:

http://gohpl.com/hudsonthehawkwhite

Once we understand the human-movement-principles, and move to analyzing video, then we must **come up with a criteria for filtering appropriate swing models**, that show a select few hitters doing the best at playing by the human-movement "rules"…

First, I want to ask you a question,

Who is your swing model?

I did an exhaustive post on this at my blog titled: *"Who Is Your Swing Model? And Why?"* Click the following link to read more on this topic:

http://gohpl.com/swingmodel

I won't go into everything discussed there, but what I did want to share is my checklist for deciding on which swings to analyze...

5 Gold Standard Criteria Keys for a High-Level Swing

You don't need to have five-out-of-five, but at least three-out-of-five:

1. **Smaller sluggers**, NO bigger than 6-feet tall, and weighing NO more than 215-pounds,
2. **Hits for both power AND average**,
3. **Above average in key Metrics** like: OPS, OPS+, HR/FB ratio, Line Drive%, Ball Exit Speed, Attack Angles, etc.,
4. **Minimal, if zero, injuries** caused by the swing over career *(in other words, the swing MUST be safe for the hitter – thank you Lee Comeaux for this one)*,
5. Understanding that big sluggers may **succeed with ineffective mechanics**, NOT because of them.

So, who are the high-level baseball-hitter-swings, I believe are the Gold Standard?

- Dustin Pedroia,
- Sadaharu Oh,
- Ted Williams *(he was 6'3", but he only weighed around 180-lbs when he broke into the league, 3rd year he hit .406 with 37 homers and 33 2B's)*,
- Hank Aaron,
- Josh Donaldson,
- Jose Bautista,
- Robinson Cano,
- Adrian Beltre,
- Mickey Mantle, and
- Andrew McCutchen.

If I were to pick one from above, it would have to be Sadaharu Oh, the Japanese baseball, **career home-run leader with 868 dingers in 20 years, standing at 5-foot, 10-inches tall, and weighing 173-pounds**.

And for my favorite fast-pitch softball hitter, who exhibits everything we cover in this book, is **Sierra Romero who's 5-foot, 5-inches tall** and CRUSHES the softball.

Can small sluggers outslug BIG ones?

Can 100-pound hitters be taught to consistently drive the ball over 300-feet?

Or said differently, can a hitter really triple their body-weight in batted ball distance?

Let's first look at some other explosive-rotational-athletes...

According to Wikipedia, here are the Olympic World Record holders for the following Olympic lifts (*in the 56Kg weight class – or 123.2-pounds*):

- **Behdad Salimi:** 216-kg Snatch (or 475.2-pounds)
- **Hossein Rezazadeh:** 263-kg Clean & Jerk (578.6-pounds)

YouTube is your friend here, so please search "Olympic Snatch" or "Olympic Clean and Jerk" to see what these lifts look like in action.

Hossein Rezazadeh 263-kg Clean & Jerk (or 578.6-pounds) weighing only 123.2-pounds. Photo by Ezra Shaw/Getty Images

Behdad lifted approximately 3.8-times his body-weight (kg) in the Snatch, and Hossein lifted approximately 4.6-times his body-weight (kg) in the Clean & Jerk (*Fig. 2 image above*).

According to Wikipedia, Ben Hogan was 5-foot, 8.5-inches, weighing 145-pounds, and some say, could consistently drive the golf ball 240-yards (720-feet), topping out at 270-yards (810-feet) downhill, and get this, with inferior technology compared to today, back in the 1940's and 50's. **What would that look like with today's technology? 300-yards? 350-yards?**

Here's what my Shot-Put friend Rob – I mentioned earlier – said in an email about Shot-Put "small boppers":

"...*nobody seems to notice that we have guys like 6'5", 325lb world champ Christian Cantwell, who benches 600lbs! And guys like National champion, 70-footer [70-foot thrower] Kevin Akins who is 6'4" 315, and squatted 850lbs!! but we also have, Dean Crouser, who weighed only 245 at 6'3", and benched only 350, and squatted only 400lbs....but Dean beat Kevin and was National Champion in 1983, throwing 69'10"....and Ed Sarul 6'1", 230lbs who won the World Championships with a throw of 70'5" beating eventual World Record holder Ulf Timmerman.*"

Or what Tim Ferriss talks about in his bestselling book, *The Four-Hour Body*, world-renowned, speed-expert, Barry Ross training one of many female track athletes, **weighing only 132-lbs, who can dead lift 400-pounds for repetitions**. She can dead lift a little over 3-times her bodyweight!

Am I getting my point across?

Can small sluggers outhit BIG ones?

Yes.

As retired Physics Professor, Alan Nathan has said, body mass isn't a good indicator of high Ball-Exit-Speeds. **Bat Speed at Impact is better indicator. If Bat Speed is low, then so will Ball-Exit-Speed**.

Can hitters triple their bodyweight in batted-ball distance? Or in the instance for softball, at least double it?

Yes…it is most certainly within the realm of possibility. Don't let Fixed Mindset coaches tell you otherwise.

To end this Chapter, I'll leave you with this…

How does a hitter like Dustin Pedroia, who according to Baseball-Reference.com, lists him at 5'9", 175-lbs, on a 162-game season average, collect 43 doubles, 15 homers, and hits .301 over 11-years in the Big Leagues?

Is it because he's gifted?

That's what some will say.

But that's a cop out.

Are you kidding me?! Gifted?! With what!!!!?

Definitely not size.

Eye-hand coordination? Better "hardware"?

Big Leaguers have above-average eye-hand coordination compared to the general population…that's one reason they've made it so far!

Better "software" and pitch recognition skills?

Maybe.

Dustin Pedroia has to be more "skilled" to compete with bigger sluggers.

Granted, physiology is only one part of the equation, but I think it's fair to say Pedroia wasn't gifted physically, like say a Giancarlo Stanton.

3

CHAPTER 3

"It's not the years in your life that count. It's the life in your years."
– Abraham Lincoln
"The more I learn, the more I realize how much I don't know."
– Albert Einstein

The Credibility Fallacy: What Makes an Effective Source of Hitting

Part of the challenge a coach, new to the hitting scene, has, is where to begin the journey.

A mentor is highly recommended.

But who do you choose?

And **how do you know if they subscribe to the human movement principles validated by science** that we're discussing here?

And where do you find him or her?

Let's clear three Credibility Fallacies in choosing the right hitting mentor online...

Do Decades Of Coaching Experience Make an Effective Hitting Coach?

One of the things Tony Robbins talks about is, if you aren't growing, then you're dying.

On the socials, if I hear a coach GLOAT that because they have 15, 20, or 30+ years of coaching experience, that should be reason enough to listen to him, then almost immediately, a red flag should go up.

If decades of coaching experience *is* THE credibility indicator, then I'd share the Lincoln quote at the start of this Chapter.

And if this coach has to gloat about that, then **he probably has the same one-year of coaching experience repeated over 30 years**.

I have a question written on my office white board that reads,

"What don't I know?"

This goes right along with the Einstein quote above.

Look, head coaches are generalists, just like CEO's are generalists.

NOT specialists.

There's a reason WHY CEO's are hired with BIG bucks to make BIG decisions, NOT small technical ones. They hire others more specialized than they are to deal with vital details like sales, technology, operations, and marketing.

Just because a head coach has more years coaching than the next person, doesn't make them an effective coach.

Why?

I want to know what they've learned about hitting each year, in all those years. And what are they "learning" now to not become the "learned".

Now, let's address the Credibility Fallacy question of...

Is Pro or MLB Playing Experience a Mark of an Effective Hitting Coach?

"So, you had how many hits in the Major Leagues???"

This is a common Fixed Mindset objection that coaches use as a filter for whose information they digest.

And I feel those who use this as priority criteria to filter hitting sources, **are dramatically missing out on knowledgeable and creative minds that GET RESULTS with their hitters**.

Shortly, I'll go into WHY this mindset is short-sighted, but for now, let's discuss how...

At least the coach with 30+ years of coaching experience has spent A LOT of teaching time in the trenches with athletes, and this is a strength.

Most likely, the ex-pro or Major League player **has not engaged in the deep, deliberate practice of teaching** since they called an end to their playing days.

Playing and coaching are two different muscles.

And each muscle gets stronger with work.

Have you heard the phrase, *"Those that can't do, teach"*?

I feel that some players "figured out feel" earlier than others, and end up higher on the level ladder.

Those left behind are **left with more questions and doubt that can drive them to dig deep and find out why they failed** and didn't move on.

This is an advantage to future coaches and instructors.

...continually asking, *"What don't I know?"*

We've all heard ex-pro, MLB, and Hall of Fame players explain how they hit – most of the time we're left scratching our heads. Their teachings more likely leave our hitters' outcomes less consistent, not more.

These professionals are teaching based on what's *feel* for them, not what's really happening on video, or what's *real*.

Again, I go back to the 2016 Mike Trout interview with Sean Casey during Spring Training, where Trout says he tries to "stay on top of the ball".

That may be his *feel*, and how he guards against "chicken winging" (in his words), but this isn't what we're seeing (what's *real*) in slow motion analysis or what his metrics reflect.

In other words, if you tell EVERY young hitter on your team to "get on top of the ball" who doesn't 'chicken wing', then most will hit an abundance of ground-balls. I'm over 90% certain of that.

But for high-level hitters like Trout, **what's *real* and what's *feel* are in a state of confusion for outsiders looking in**.

Just like with coaches having quite a few years under their belt, with ex-pro and MLB players, I disregard playing experience as a credibility indicator to being successful coaching hitters.

What matters in the coaching world are the results your hitters experience. And this is a direct reflection of the process used to get them those outcomes. The latter being more important.

A good example is Barry Bonds getting let go as the Florida Marlins hitting coach after the 2016 season. At the current time of this writing, he's the MLB career home run leader, and PED use aside, Bonds was putting up outstanding numbers before that period in his career.

So why did the Marlins let him go?

From USAToday.com:

"Miami finished fourth in the majors in batting average at .263 but fourth-lowest in runs at 655 and next-to-last with 128 homers. The Marlins improved in all three categories from 2015."

In addition, the BIGFOOT, Giancarlo Stanton was a mere mortal offensively in 2016.

I just think **Barry Bonds cannot translate and apply to other players how he did what he did when he played**.

The bottom line?

Playing experience is virtually irrelevant in the coaching world. It can land you a job, but then producing hitters that consistently crush with authority is what it will take to KEEP that job.

And one last thing,

How about the guy who uses the fact he was an MLB hitting coach at some point in his career?

I turn to *Positional Hitting* book author Jaime Cevallos for the answer to this:

*"**MLB hitting coaches are motivated by keeping their job, not developing innovative principles.** If they change a franchise player's swing, and that player gets worse, their name is forever blacklisted. Word will spread that he makes good hitters bad. And regardless of how many hitters he has helped, the one he "ruined" will be the bane of his career. GMs will attach his name with money flying out the window. He can just take a seat next to Jose Canseco in the list of people who will never be offered a contract. Because of this, **MLB hitting coaches develop vague hitting methods, appearing to help when the team is doing well, yet standing on no specific method when the team is struggling.** It's common for them to wait until a player on the team gets hot, and associate themselves to that player as much as possible. I've seen it time and time again."*

What about "That Guy" on the socials who says…

"Spending 'years' in cages is what makes you a great coach."

I wanted to address the coach who gloats they've spent a ton of time in the cages, and that makes him an authority on hitting.

Listen, what if you set out to break the Guinness Book of World Records by climbing the world's tallest building.

And you're convinced it's the One World Trade Center in New York, New York.

But when you get to the top…

You find out last minute by double-checking Google, that the tallest building IS NOT the One World Trade Center, but the Burj Khalifa located in Dubai.

All that work, for nothing.

You just climbed the WRONG building chief. How does that make you feel?

Putting years of hitting lessons into the cages, watching millions of hours of slow-motion video footage of who you think are "only the best hitters", coupled with 30+ years of coaching DOES NOT make you an authority on hitting.

What does?

…And this brings us back to who does a new hitting coach listen to…

How well the hitting source understands human-movement-principles that are validated by science. REAL science. NOT pseudo-science.

If a coach is pointed in the right direction, then all the other things mentioned in this Chapter fall into place.

Who is Joey Myers?

Am I just bitter that I didn't play pro-ball?

Am I covering up the fact that I don't have 30+ years of coaching experience?

Am I feeling less-than-manly because I haven't accumulated 30,000 lessons in the past year?

Or, am I lazy because I don't want to spend millions of hours sitting behind a computer screen watching slow-motion analysis video?

The following has been copy and pasted from the HittingPerformanceLab.com About Me page…

"My Name is Joey Myers, and I'm the founder of the Hitting Performance Lab. I'm a member of the **American Baseball Coaches Association (ABCA)**, the **International Youth and Conditioning Association (IYCA)**, and the **Society for American Baseball Research (SABR)**. I'm also a huge supporter of the **Positive Coaching Alliance (PCA)**.

I'm a certified Youth Fitness Specialist (YFS) through the International Youth Conditioning Association (IYCA), Corrective Exercise Specialist (CES) through the National Academy of Sports Medicine (NASM), and Vinyasa yoga instructor…AND, I'm also certified in the Functional Muscle Screen (FMS).

And by the time you read this, I may have my Practitioner and Masters certification in the NLP, or Neuro-Linguistic Programming. The basis of what Tony Robbins teaches.

I've spent 11+ years in the corrective fitness field, and have a **passionate curiosity to help other players – just like you and your hitters – dramatically improve performance through the science of human movement**.

But it wasn't so long ago that I was just as frustrated as your hitters are now. The stats I accumulated in my four years of Division One baseball at Fresno State (2000-2003) were completely sub-par:

.250 AVG, 9 homers, and 40 RBIs

I'm sure you'll agree that these aren't exactly impressive stats. I DON'T analyze thousands of hours of video footage. I DON'T spend 16 hours a day doing hitting lessons. I DON'T even have 30+ years of coaching experience!

Remember, **it's not the years of experience…it's the experience in your years**.

What I've found, is that playing resumes don't mean a DARN THING in the coaching world. They may get you the job, but it's results that count. Results with real hitters. Here is a handful of my first crop of hitters getting results that were exposed early to the principles in this book:

- 98-lb, 11yo hitting the ball 300-feet, multiple times,
- 95-pounder hitting their first dinger over 270-feet (this is actually the brother of the above hitter, but 2 years younger),
- 135-lb 13yo hitting the ball 370-feet multiple times,
- **66-lb 11yo hitting the ball over 180-feet**, and…
- Another 135-lb 13yo hitting the ball 360-feet.

By the way, these are just MY hitters. **I have thousands of coaches across the United States that apply**

the same HPL principles and get similar results – if not better! I've received multiple weekly emails from coaches/instructors/parents since January of 2013 that tell me so.

Just as Chas Pippitt of BaseballRebellion.com so elegantly put it, when given the Fixed Mindset coaching challenge, *"So, you had how many hits in the Major Leagues???"* – Chas is a friend that puts in a lot of hours in the cages and gets outstanding results with his hitters. Thanks Chas for the following response, it's classic…

*"Just like Stephen Hawking, a world leader on black holes, I've never been to outer space…Just like Bill Belichick, I have never played in the NFL…Idan Ravin works with Chris Paul, Lebron James, Melo on basketball skill training…and he's never even played COLLEGE ball…Just like Rudy Jaramillo, one of the top hitting coaches in the bigs ever, I have no MLB playing experience…***Dave Duncan, widely considered one of the best pitching coaches ever…was a catcher."*

The bottom line is this…

It's NOT how you study, but what you study that counts. We apply human-movement-principles that are validated by science to hitting a ball. Physicists…Biologists…Bio-mechanical Engineers…and Body Workers.

For example, on earth, you'll fall 100% of the time skydiving out of a plane, right?! Because of Gravitational Forces! **Our knowledge of human-movement-principles may refine, but NEVER change and remain constant.**

I've had multiple hitters and families come to hit with me in Fresno, CA from:

- San Diego (6.5 hour drive one-way),
- Los Angeles (4-hour drive one-way),
- San Francisco & Bay Area (3-hour drive one-way),
- Sacramento (3.5-hour drive one-way),
- Boston (5-hour plane flight one-way), and
- Canada (3-5 hour plane flight one-way)…

And the common thing they tell me, is that nobody in their area is teaching hitting from a human-movement-principle perspective, validated by science.

So, NO, I'm not bitter that I didn't play pro-ball. I was mentally burned out after college ball anyway.

NO, I don't need to cover up the fact that I don't have 30+ years of coaching experience.

NO, I don't feel less-than-manly because I haven't accumulated 30,000 lessons in the past year.

And finally, NO, I'm not lazy because I don't want to spend millions of hours sitting behind a computer screen watching slow-motion analysis video.

I love to work hard. Anyone who knows me will tell you that. **I just like to work smarter on being more effective. There's only so much head banging against the wall I can take!**

Just as President Lincoln said,

"It's not the years in your life that count. It's the life in your years."

…that makes you an authority.

Now, let's look into how to speed up the learning curve when wading through the muck that is hitting philosophy and theory…

4

CHAPTER 4

*"I spend a lot of time talking to people who disagree with me – I would go so far as to say that it's my favorite leisure activity – **and repeatedly I meet individuals who are eager to share their views on science, despite the fact that they have never done an experiment**. They have never tested an idea for themselves, using their own hands, or seen the results of that test, using their own eyes, and they have never thought carefully about what those results mean for the idea they are testing, using their own brain. To these people, "science" is a monolith, a mystery, and an authority, rather than a method."*
– Ben Goldacre, book: *Bad Science: Quacks, Hacks, & Big Pharma Flacks*

How & WHY to Do Swing Experiments

To view my full swing-experiment blueprint, CLICK the following blog link:
   http://gohpl.com/swingexperiment
   Before I get into how to conduct an effective swing-experiment…
   I want to show how NOT to do one…
   My first exposure to swing-experiments occurred when I was in the 6th grade and I was 11 or 12 years old.
   For school, **one of my best friends and I were required to conduct an experiment using the Scientific Method**.
   Because we both LOVED baseball and hitting, we decided to test metal versus wood bats. We would test which bat would hit the ball the farthest.
   We used one wood bat, and each of us used our own metals, an Easton and Louisville Slugger. All bats were different sizes and weights.
   We then took turns throwing batting practice to each other using each of the three bats. We'd both hit about 10-20 balls with each bat.
   For example, I'd hit 15 balls with the wood bat, then my friend would hit 15. Then we'd measure the batted ball distance and repeat for the other bats. **Probably, the ONLY smart thing we did in this experiment**.
   We hit between 50-100 balls, I can't remember because it was so long ago.

And get this…we measured off the distance using the "stepping method", which was a problem because at the time I wore about a Men's size 10, and my buddy a Men's 13!

MORONS!!

And guess what our hypothesis was, along with probably most of the US population?

We figured the metal would outperform wood.

Duh!

However, do you know which bat "won" in our experiment?

Wood!

Now, let me ask you, what do you think our teacher thought of our experiment?

She was kind enough to give us a "C"!!

So, what could we have done better?

The following tweaks would have made this experiment an "A+":

- Use the same length, weight, and MOI (moment of inertia*) wood and metal bat.
- Use 1 metal, 1 wood…not 2 metals, and 1 wood.
- **Instead of THROWING batting practice, we should have hit off a tee, positioned in the same point of contact for all swings.**
- Get more data points, or plan to hit 200 balls between my friend and I (I take 100 swings – 50 with each bat, he takes 100 swings – 50 with each bat).
- Counter-balance the swings, to take out the "getting warmed up" and "getting tired" biases (*I'll explain later in this chapter*).
- And most importantly, we should have measured, not "stepping off" the distance with our different sized feet, but with a **rolling tape measure wheel along a straight line of red colored yarn string from the** "blast zone" to the end range of the batted ball.

Moment of inertia (or MOI) is a fancy term describing the center mass of bat location. Basically, if you tried to balance the bat length-wise between a pinched thumb and forefinger, where would the balance point be? Some bats are referred to as "top-heavy" or "well-balanced". This is MOI in a nutshell.

Importance of Isolating the Variable

One of the two biggest themes I learned in doing swing experiments is **the importance of isolating the variable**. And in our case, was the performance of the two bats, metal versus wood.

Different weights, lengths, and MOI's can have a profound impact on the data collected.

For instance, a "top heavy" bat is more likely to outperform a "balance-weighted" bat in Ball-Exit-Speed. Not as much with differing bat lengths and weights. This is according to retired Physics Professor, Dr. Alan Nathan.

Recently, I received the following Facebook comment from a coach about one of my swing-experiments:

"There are a couple variables that I don't think relate to 'Live Performance'…

1. Hitting was done without any forward move.
2. The controlled environment doesn't take into account the most important part of being a good hitter…vision to see and hit a moving target.

If we are talking about golf, then I would feel more agreeable. There are other 'Live' factors not mentioned in this. I believe usable power comes from:

The Pitcher's Velo, having good timing, staying short with as much separation as possible (everyone is different), getting in the weight room!"

The comment was on a post revisiting the original 'Showing the Numbers' swing experiment, which we'll go over in CHAPTER 8.

And don't get me wrong, I agree wholeheartedly with this coach, however, **not in an experiment setting when we're attempting to isolate a variable**.

Here's why...

In the experiment, we broke the 200 swings into two chunks...

> 1. Get to landing position, pause for a second or two, and then
> 2. Swing.

The reason for this was to make sure we were 'NOT showing' OR 'showing numbers' on the swings we were supposed to. The hitter taking the swings, typically showed his numbers well, so when 'NOT showing' them; **it would have been a challenge with a full cut to execute properly**.

This addressed the 'done without a forward move' comment.

Now, to address the "LIVE factors"...

Our goal in this experiment was to see the difference in Ball-Exit-Speed – and other swing metrics – when a hitter showed or didn't show their numbers.

That hitting mechanic was the variable, so we MUST isolate it.

Just like with my first swing-experiment, introducing a LIVE pitch can really muddle the experiment findings, namely:

- Differing pitch velocities, and
- Differing pitch locations.

Both of these bring in vision, tracking, and timing elements, and unless this was part of the experiment, **they are irrelevant and not useful to our objective**.

My comment was that if we had tested 'showing numbers' versus 'NOT showing numbers' against a LIVE pitcher, and captured Ball-Exit-Speed, we would have had a 15 to 25-mph jump in BES...instead of 9-mph when 'Showing Numbers' hitting off a batting tee.

It's like reducing fractions...2/6ths becomes 1/3.

The point is, **we want to isolate the variable the best we can, so we can compare apples to apples**.

Besides, Bat Speed and Ball-Exit-Speed have a more dramatic effect on batted ball distance than pitching velocity does. The numbers break down like this:

- 1-mph of pitching velocity ADDS 1-foot of batted ball distance,
- 1-mph of Ball-Exit-Speed ADDS 4-feet of batted ball distance, and in general
- If Bat Speeds are low, then so will Ball-Exit-Speeds.

Keeping Objectivity

The other theme I learned in doing swing-experiments is to maintain objectivity. In other words, being a good journalist, reporting equal facts on both sides, and being as neutral as possible on the subject being tested.

I'm going to quote objectivity from...

Dr. Richard Feynman, an American theoretical physicist, worked on Manhattan Project, received the Nobel Prize in Physics in 1965, British journal Physics World said he was ranked as one of the ten greatest physicists of all time, NY Times bestselling author to the book, *"Surely, You're Joking Mr. Feynman!"* says this about maintaining an objective nature (and I'm paraphrasing here):

"Give people all the facts they need to judge the value of your contribution, not just info that leads to judgment into one outcome or another. Be careful of biases."

The problem the hitting industry has faced over the last few decades, is the idea of pseudo-science, or what Dr. Richard Feynman calls "Cargo-Cult-Science" …

Cargo-Cult-Science as defined by Dr. Feynman in his book:

*"In the South Seas there is a cargo cult of people. During the war, they saw airplanes land with lots of good materials, and they want the same thing to happen now. So, they've arranged to imitate things like runways, to put fires along the sides of the runways, to make a wooden hut for a man to sit in, with two wooden pieces on his head like headphones and bars of bamboo sticking out like antennas—he's the controller—and they wait for the airplanes to land. **They're doing everything right. The form is perfect. It looks exactly the way it looked before. But it doesn't work.** No airplanes land. So, I call these things cargo-cult-science, because they follow all the apparent precepts and forms of scientific investigation, but they're missing something essential, because the planes don't land."*

Thanks to today's technology we can make the seemingly immeasurable…measurable.

Zepp, SwingTracker by Diamond Kinetics, and Blast Motion are great investments for coaches to measure Bat Speed at Impact, Attack Angle, Hand Speed Max, and Time to Impact…to name just a few.

If a coach wants to measure Ball-Exit-Speed, then they can do so, sitting behind the hitter with a Bushnell Radar Gun, or PocketRadar.

Sure, there are fancy solutions like HitTrax that can do it all plus some, but you'll spend a fortune.

The point is, **we coaches can now put mechanics to the test and find out what is effective and what is not**. Gone are the days coaches engage in online-forum pissing contests, debating hitting philosophy and theory.

I first published the swing-experiment-blueprint link *(included at the beginning of this Chapter)* on June 12, 2015, and at the end asked coaches to:

"Post your baseball/softball hitting experiment results below in the comments section"…

However, all I've heard are crickets.

Why would this be?

I understand that the mom or dad shelling out $80-150 for a Zepp or SwingTracker may be a little much.

But for the Academies, instructors, and online hitting experts who do this for a living, this kind of money shouldn't be a challenge.

From this CHAPTER, you now know how to do swing-experiments, so that excuse cannot be used.

Not enough time?

Could be.

But I think it goes deeper…

My friend, Bryan Eisenberg (@TheGrok on Twitter) offered a solution that may explain things…

I shared my frustration with him about this, and he said, Joey, it **may be because most self-proclaimed hitting gurus are scared what the experiments will reveal about their own teachings**.

In other words, it could show they're teaching an inferior model.

Like my great friend, Ken Carswell said from KCHitter.com, who is an expert in distraction training for hitters:

"There's nothing more fragile than the 40-year-old male ego."

Conducting validating or invalidating swing experiments do require checking your ego at the door.

If you're a hitting coach out there with a Growth Mindset, then you won't have a problem doing this.

Conducting swing-experiments will change the way you think about hitting.

You see,

The problem with hitting philosophy and theory is the large amount of uncertainty.

The goal that I have for the end of this Chapter is to challenge you coaches to adopt some sort of swing experimentation in your practice.

Use my swing-experiment-blueprint as a jumping-off point on how to do them, and improve upon it.

Invest in some of the swing measuring equipment mentioned earlier.

Learn from some of the mistakes I illustrated at the start of this Chapter, and please share your swing-experiment results in the comments section of the following link:

http://gohpl.com/swingexperiment

"Go forth and make awesomeness" – unknown

5

CHAPTER 5

"The axial rotation of the spine cannot happen unless the spine is flexed by the right amount on the correct side. Coaching an athlete to throw without a proper spinal position is an invitation to severe torsional injuries."
– Dr. Serge Gracovetsky, Physicist and Electrical Engineer

The Science of Repeatable Power

We're now going to dig into the science of how and why *The Catapult Loading System* is a more effective, and safe alternative to what's currently being taught in mainstream hitting circles.

You are free to skip this Chapter if you don't want to get into the weeds.

But later on, when your hitters are crushing the ball, you'll want to **come back and read it because you'll need something to explain to Fixed Mindset coaches who won't believe how your hitters are doing what they're doing**.

I promise to make this material as palatable as possible.

What follows is a boiled down version, from all my research and study, of springy fascia and the Spinal Engine. Most of what I'll be talking about on these topics came from Thomas Myers' book *Anatomy Trains* and Dr. Serge Gracovetsky's book *The Spinal Engine*.

As Albert Einstein once said,

"Everything should be made as simple as possible, but no simpler."

The Power of Springy Fascia

To start off this lesson, I want to run you through a physical experiment…

I assume you're sitting down in a chair or on a couch reading this book.

If you aren't, then you'll need to sit down for this.

Place your right hand, palm down on the Good Book, the Bible, and repeat after me…

Kidding!

Okay seriously, place your right hand, palm down, on your right thigh.

If you're left-handed, then please reverse the following instructions…

Now, with the rest of your fingers keeping contact with your leg, I want you to lift up your right index finger (pointer), and slam it down on your thigh as hard as you can three times.

Notice the force of the finger striking your leg.

This is an example of using only muscle to propel the finger down.

Next, keeping the rest of your fingers in contact with your leg, I want you to pull your right index finger back as far as you can, using your left hand, and without trying to slam it down, let go of the finger letting it crack down on your thigh.

Note the different feeling of force at the surface of your leg.

This is using only springy fascia to release the finger's stored energy.

Lastly, and again keeping the rest of your fingers in contact with your thigh, I want you to pull your right index finger back as far as you can using your left hand, and at the same time you release the finger like before, slam the finger down.

Note the different down smashing force felt on the thigh from the same finger.

This is using both springy fascia and muscle to whack the thigh with the finger.

Like I mentioned earlier in the book, most hitting experts understand the function of muscle, and base their primary teachings on its use.

However, as you can see in our little physical experiment, **there was more force applied by making the finger springy** (pulling finger back and letting it catapult down)…and even more force when springy and muscle forces were combined.

Here are some key elements to fascia, pronounced like "Fash-a":So, what is this springy force made up of?

It's a form of connective tissue similar to a knee ACL/MCL or Achilles tendon:

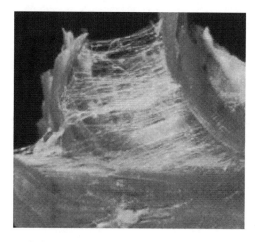

- **Like cotton candy or a spider web like material**
- Is what our bones and muscles *float* in
- Gives muscles their shape
- Is made up of mostly collagen fibers and some elastin (collagen is the same material Hollywood stuffs into their faces)
- Collagen is 100 times more stiff than elastin
- Is to the human body, like steel is to the building industry (very good at resisting changes in shape)
- **Is like a 'glue' that ties all tissues of the body together**. On AnatomyTrains.com, Myers poses the question: "Are there really 600 muscles or only one muscle in 600 fascial pockets?"
- When stretching in the morning, you're

Fascia is a cotton candy or spider webby like material. Photo courtesy: AnatomyTrains.com

'smoothing out' the "fascial fuzz" build up from a night of non-movement. This is why a wide array of movement is so crucial to keeping your fascia healthy

When we walk, experts say the Achilles tendon acts like a 'catapult' propelling us forward…hence, is where *The Catapult Loading System* was derived.

According to Thomas Myers in his book, *Anatomy Trains*, the 'Fascial Net' is made up of opposing compression and tension forces that act within the body at all times. Myers calls this Tensegrity, or Tension-Integrity.

A Compression force is like two bricks laying one on top of the other. The top brick exerts a pressure down, thanks to Gravity, on the brick below it.

Relating to the body, this can be illustrated as the bones stacked on top of each other with slabs of meat (the muscle) wrapping on top of and around the bone adding more compressive weight.

Tension is like a boom crane with a swinging wrecking ball hanging from a cable. The tension between the heavy ball and the structure of the boom crane is felt in the cable connecting the two.

Tying together the importance of both compression and tension forces, let's look at a rock you may be familiar with, granite.

Granite is one of the most compression-resistant rocks on earth. However, if you hooked up two horses, by rope, on opposite ends of a slab, and had them create tension and pull the Granite apart, it's one of the weakest stones on earth when it comes to resisting tension.

The human body uses both tension and compression, equally well.

Manipulating these opposing tension and compression forces of fascia is where consistent power is found.

So how do these compression and tension forces work?

The Springy 'X' Pattern

I walk you through this concept using Adrian Gonzalez's swing as an example at the following link:

http://gohpl.com/springyx

In addition, CLICK the next link if you want to see the difference in Springy 'X' Pattern between Ted Williams and Matt Kemp:

http://gohpl.com/williamspringyx

The following description can be confirmed by reading the Thomas Myers book *Anatomy Trains*. The Chapters to focus on in his book would be:

- Front Arm Lines,
- Back Arm Lines,
- Lateral Lines,
- Functional Lines, and
- The Spiral Lines.

All eight of the fascial lines Myers traces, affect each other and interweave, but those five primarily make up loading the Springy 'X' Pattern.

Now, I want you to…

Imagine one red 'X' painted on your chest and another one painted on your back. Each leg of the 'X' connects one shoulder to the opposite hip.

In order to optimize the springiness of fascia, we have to shorten one leg of the 'X', while lengthening the other.

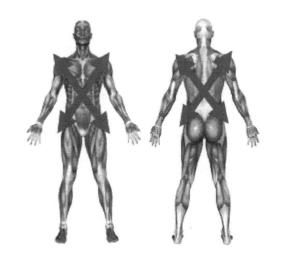

Imagine a red 'X' painted on your chest and back connecting your opposite hip and shoulder…

The same can be said for both the chest and back, but each leg of the 'X' is reversed.

Let me explain…

Let's use a righty-hitter, say Josh Donaldson for example.

You lefties out there, please reverse the following instructions.

Before Josh Donaldson lands his stride foot, we'll see him bring his front shoulder down and in towards his back hip, SHORTENING that leg of the chest 'X'. And for you, fast-pitch softball coaches, substitute Sierra Romero for Josh Donaldson…she does this really well.

He's doing what I cue to my hitters as:

- **Showing his numbers to the pitcher** (on his back), and
- **Getting a slight downhill shoulder angle**.

And at the same time, the other leg of the 'X', on the chest, connecting his front hip to his back shoulder will LENGTHEN because we'll see him "hide his hands from the pitcher".

This is also what we see when a boxer loads up a knockout punch.

Did I lose you yet?

Stay with me, to recap so far:

- As close to stride landing as possible, Josh Donaldson is shortening the front shoulder to back hip leg of the chest 'X', and
- Lengthening the front hip to back shoulder leg of the chest 'X'.

On the back, the legs of the 'X' reverse in relation to the front.

So, as the front shoulder to opposite hip leg of the chest 'X' shortens, the same line connecting the two same points on the back, lengthen.

The same is true for the lengthening of the front hip to opposite shoulder leg of the chest 'X', the same line tracing on the back, shortens.

I simplify the concept by tracing an effective *Catapult Loading System* by following the movement of the front shoulder: **Once the hitter's turn has initiated, we'll see all shortening and lengthening legs of the 'X' reverse.**

- We will see Donaldson's left shoulder start down and in, as close to stride landing as possible,

My 13yo 135-pound lefty consistently pounding the ball 370-feet. Flipped swing to show righty example.

My lefty (turned righty) example of the 'X' leg reversal during turn.

- Then during the turn, we'll see his left shoulder go up and away, and
- Finally, during follow through we will see his left shoulder finish down and in. **Think of the famous swing finishes of Ted Williams or Lou Gehrig.**

The legs of the springy 'X' have reversed yet again, and have almost returned to normal length.

In the final stages of the swing, we'll see the shoulders return to their beginning starting place but flipped.

Described above are snapshots of the process, so please understand the shoulders are transitioning between these still mental images.

One last point I want to leave you with before moving onto the science of the Spinal Engine, has to do with…

Red Kangaroos and Springy Fascia

The Red Kangaroo.

I bet you didn't think, in a book about hitting, you'd being learning about kangaroos?!! lol

Oh, how talking hitting principles is GREAT!

Quoted from a review titled, *"Energetics and biomechanics of locomotion by red kangaroos"*, by Rodger Kram and Terence J. Dawson from CBP (Comparative Biochemistry & Physiology) reported that…

Red Kangaroo. Photo courtesy: Wikipedia.org

*"As red kangaroos hop faster over ground level, their rate of oxygen consumption (indicating metabolic energy consumption) remains nearly the same. **This phenomenon has been attributed to exceptional elastic energy storage and recovery via long compliant tendons in the legs."***

What does this mean?

The faster a Red Kangaroo hops over level ground, the less energy they need.

WHY?

Whether we're talking fascia, connective tissue, or tendons…we're essentially talking about the same thing. They're made up of the same mix of elastin and collagen fibers – but mostly collagen.

Fascia DOES NOT need external energy sources, like food, to run optimally. Unlike our muscles, which require thousands of calories per day to move.

The above Red Kangaroo Review is also a great example of tendons acting like a "catapult" again, hence *The Catapult Loading System*.

Look, just like in our finger snap test earlier, **the swing should not be just springy fascia, or just muscle...it should be a mix of both**. Contrary to this, most hitting theory out there, errors on the side of muscle ONLY.

Now, I'd like to dive into the benefits of the Spinal Engine as described by Dr. Serge Gracovetsky in his book, *The Spinal Engine*...

The Science of the Spinal Engine

What follows is a brief Anatomy lesson about the spine. I promise to make it as painless as possible.

Here are three main pieces of the spine:

- **Neck** – Cervical (C-Spine)
- **Mid to Upper Back** – Thoracic (T-Spine)
- **Lower Back** – Lumbar (L-Spine)

Imagine for a moment the letter 'C' (the lower-back portion)...

Then picture another 'C' turned upside down on top of first 'C' (the mid-to-upper-back portion)...

And lastly, imagine another 'C' turned upside down on top of the third 'C' (the neck portion).

Imagine an 'S' making up all three 'C' pieces.

What's more…

Both the bottom and middle 'C' sections move opposite each other, lower-back portion controls the pelvis, and the mid-to-upper-back portion controls the shoulders.

The neck portion of the spine can move independently of both the low-back & mid-to-upper back sections.

This is WHY our opposite arm and leg come forward when we walk or run.

Now, let's talk about the…

3 Motions of the Spine

Have you ever watched TV lying upside down?

…Like kids do on the couch sometimes?

I have!

Yes, my wife hasn't quite gotten over the fact I'm a little weird, but what's cool is, my kids haven't!! lol

What you'll notice when watching television upside down is people seem to bounce when they walk.

What's happening here?

A couple things…

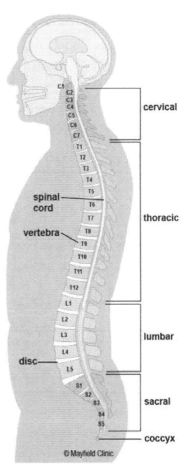

Anatomy of the Spine. Photo courtesy: MayFieldClinic.com

According to Dr. Serge Gracovetsky, in his book, *The Spinal Engine*, the Physicist reveals three motions of the spine:

> 1. **Flexion/Extension** (Google Hollow Position or Upward-Facing Dog Pose),
> 2. **Lateral Flexion** (bending sideways at the waist), and
> 3. **Axial Rotation** (when the shoulders twist opposite the pelvis – known to some as torque).

Dr. Gracovetsky then adds that if two of the above are present, then almost always the end result is the third. This is called the Coupled Motion of the spine.

Watch about 4-minutes of the following YouTube video where Dr. Serge Gracovetsky describes the Coupled Motion of the spine, and come on back…

http://gohpl.com/drsergespinalengine

What's interesting to note in that video is the ongoing tail wagging the dog debate…

Whether it's the spine engine driving the action of the arms and legs or it's the arms and leg action driving the actions of the spine.

So, it's the dog wagging the tail, NOT the other way around. Dr. Gracovetsky shows us a quadriplegic walking across the ground in his isocheim (bottom of pelvis). This gentleman was born without arms and legs, yet **if you were to cover up where his legs would be and watch him move, his spinal movement looks EXACTLY like that of a person with arms and legs!**

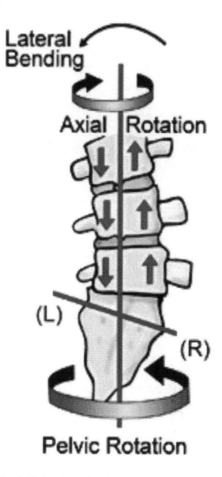

Coupled Motion of the spine. Photo courtesy: ErikDalton.com

What does this mean?

The Spinal Engine is what drives ALL human movement, not the arms and legs.

The arms and legs just amplify the action of the Spinal Engine.

Another question may be…

Does Gravity drive the Spinal Engine?

Quite a few hitting instructors promote the swing starts from the ground up.

I respectfully disagree…

In a May 24, 2014 email response to me from Dr. Gracovetsky about this, he said:

"The coupled motion has nothing to do with gravity. It works in space as well. It is a property of the spine or any flexible rod for that matter.

But the interaction with gravity makes interesting results which are exploited by every sport."

In other words, legs ARE NOT necessary for locomotion, they're an enhancement to it.

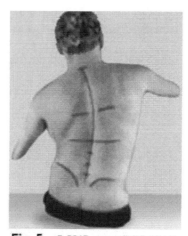

Born quadriplegic patient demos spinal engine. Photo courtesy: Erikdalton.com

On that earth-shattering note, we'll move into the application part of *The Catapult Loading System.* The fun stuff…

Hooray! You made it out of the weeds!

6

CHAPTER 6

*"How to hit home runs: I swing as hard as I can, and I try to swing right through the ball... **The harder you grip the bat, the more you can swing it through the ball, and the farther the ball will go.** I swing big, with everything I've got. I hit big or I miss big. I like to live as big as I can."*
– Babe Ruth

Finger Pressure: The Bat Drag Killer

Did you know…?

Our brains have saved something like 47% of motor-learning space for our hands? (*Thanks Lee Comeaux for this fun fact!*)

This is one reason 'taking the hands to the ball' can be a deadly coaching cue to an aspiring effective swing.

My Sophomore year in High School was the first year I made the Varsity team, playing Freshman ball the year before.

In that second year, I was graced to play every game, getting most every at-bat, while only hitting .250 with extra base hits being limited to doubles and the occasional triple.

I was lucky to hit it to the fence on the fly.

I don't mean to brag, but my slightly above average speed and routes in center-field were WHY I played that whole year, because it definitely wasn't my hitting.

However, that next summer, before starting my Junior year, I made a small change in my swing that proved to be dramatically contrary to the hitting outcomes I had experienced during the school year.

I can't remember whether I was tinkering, and figured it out, or my coach suggested it…

All I know is, that IT WORKED!!

Thinking back on it now, I was ignorance on FIRE.

What I did was swing tight with my top hand, and relax the bottom hand.

The results?

That summer I ended up hitting over .400, and hitting my first 2 or 3 High School homers!

I'm not aware of any other specific changes mechanically…

…no change in the bat I used…

…no change in strength and/or body-weight or size…

…mind you, this happened on the heels of my school season, which had about a two-week gap from Summer Legion ball.

What I call now as Finger Pressure, was the difference.

During that summer, I remember whenever I'd take a bad cut in the middle of an at-bat, and I'd look down to my coach for signs in the third base coaching box, **he'd squeeze his right hand tight, and shake out his left hand – because I'm a righty – to remind me to stay with the finger pressure process.**

Let's just say, my coach was quite happy with the end results.

My Junior and Senior years, I ended up hitting .398 both years with a handful of dingers and a ton of doubles on a field that was quite large…330-feet down the lines, 405-feet to straight away center, and about 365-feet in the gaps.

WHY did this work so well?

Hand Tension like Babe Ruth

Fast forward to March of 2015, to a swing-experiment that I did at the following link:

http://gohpl.com/handtensionexperiment

I wanted to see what happened to Bat Speed at Impact and Hand Speed Max when using, what I called at the time, hand tension versus relaxed hands.

Taking 100 swings both ways, so 200 swings total, I found:

- **+3 mph average bat speed**
- Higher Max Bat Speed numbers
- More horizontal bat angle at impact (matching pitch plane)
- **+6 degrees in attack angle**
- More productive outcomes (line-drives & fly-balls).

The coaching cue I used for hand tension was to "**break the handle between the hands**". I told the hitter to start this when they pick up their front foot to start their swing.

This flies in the face of what I was taught growing up…

I was taught that loose hands are quick hands, so why the dramatic difference in the above experiment numbers?

An Ah-ha Moment: The Evolution of Hand Tension

Well, I would later run into my now good friend and mentor Lee Comeaux.

Lee knows golf, instructing professional and non-professional golfers…some traveling from Australia and Germany to work with him in Texas.

You have to understand that Lee has been digesting Thomas Myers's book *Anatomy Trains* a good 8 years longer than I have.

In a chat with him on the phone, he was ranting about "finger pressure".

This brought me back to three things I had come across at the time…

First, it drew me back to my 'ignorance on fire' experience the summer before my Junior year in High School story.

Second, I had just listened to a podcast where host, Tim Ferriss, interviewed famous kettle bell strength and conditioning coach, Pavel Tsatsouline. In the interview, Pavel talked about **how the hands can be used to recruit more muscle tissue and connect larger areas of the body.**

And the last thing had to do with Homer Kelly, who wrote the book: *The Golfing Machine.*

Homer Kelly was an aeronautical engineer for Boeing during the Great Depression, fell in love with golf, and applied engineering principles to his golf swing.

In the book, specifically, Homer Kelly talks about four power accumulators…and for our purposes with Finger Pressure, the first power accumulator said this (p.70 in the 7th edition):

"…is the Bent Right Arm – the Hitter's Muscle Power Accumulator. Even though the Right Biceps is active, the Backstroke is always made with the Right Arm striving to remain straight. But **the straight Left Arm restraints this continuous Extensor Action of the right triceps** *with an effortless Checkering Action. Consequently, during Release, the Right Arm can straighten only as the Left Arm moves away from the Right Shoulder. This results in a smooth, even Thrust For acceleration of the Lever Assemblies from an otherwise unruly force."*

Mr. Kelly is describing a right-handed golfer in the above.

Notice the opposing tension between both hands and arms?

So, as Lee rants on about Finger Pressure, it's no wonder this idea clicks for me.

This neural association pump was already well primed in my mind.

The Science of Finger Pressure

What part of the hand do you lead with in hammering a nail?

Which part of the hand would you prefer to use if you had to break a cinderblock, block of ice, or board to have a best chance of not breaking your hand?

Most likely, you'd use the bottom. Namely, the pinky, ring, and middle fingers.

Now, which fingers do you use to:

- Write with?
- Hold chopsticks?
- Brush your teeth? Or
- If you were a surgeon and had to weld a sharp scalpel on a brain?

Most likely, you'd use the thumb, forefinger (pointer), and middle fingers.

There's a reason we're made this way…

Well, according to Thomas Myers's book, *Anatomy Trains*, there are two arm fascial lines, the Front and Back.

Imagine standing with your feet shoulder-width apart with straight arms raised to your sides, palms facing forward, and hands shoulder height.

If you trace the Front Arm Lines, then they'd run from the pinky, ring, and middle fingers across the bottom of the forearm, triceps, chest, and connect to the other side using the same route.

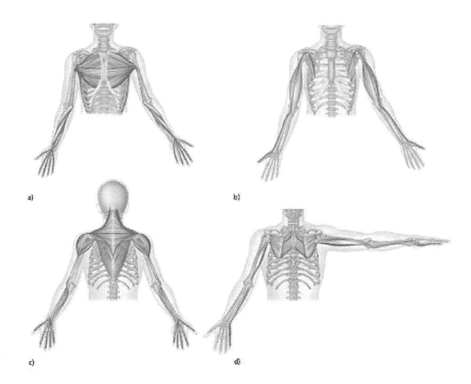

Front & Back Arm Lines. Photo courtesy: study-group-tomiki-aikido.wikispaces.com

This is considered the power part of the hand and arm.

If you trace the Back Arm Lines, then they'd run from the thumb, pointer, and middle fingers across the top of the forearm, biceps, upper back, and connect to the other side using the same route.

The Back Arm Line connection is where dexterity and precision are found.

These fascial lines are also reflexive…so if the bottom part of the hand is associated with power, then so is the outside part of the foot, pinky, ring, and "middle" toes.

The big toe, "pointer", and "middle" are the precision part.

If you watch Usain Bolt run at 10,000 frames-per-second on YouTube, you'll see the outside part of both feet slightly down more than the inside part.

The other interesting thing to note with fascia, according to Thomas Myers, is **the synovial fluid inside our joints is a liquid at rest.**

Imagine waiting for a throw from a partner while playing catch…

The moment that ball hits the glove, you squeeze the hand, wrist, forearm, and arm muscles, and as a result, the synovial fluid momentarily turns solid.

The same can be said for a hitter's grip at impact.

The main point I want you to get though, has more to do with **how Top Hand, Bottom Three-Finger Pressure connects the bat a hitter is swinging to the fascial lines interweaved throughout the turning torso.**

And this is where Finger Pressure KILLS bat drag…

How to Eliminate Racing Back Elbow Bat Drag in Two-Weeks

What is racing back elbow bat drag?

It's when the back elbow of the top hand races passed the hands before impact.

The hitting outcomes associated with this nasty bugger are weak fly balls to the opposite side of the diamond, and ground-balls to the pull side.

WHY?

Since the back elbow gets out in front of the hands, this **drops the barrel too low and this is where the weak fly balls stem from**.

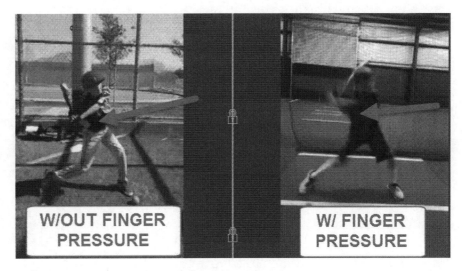

This is my 11yo 67-pounder that can hit the ball 180-feet. BEFORE finger pressure and AFTER.

For every action, there's an opposite and equal reaction...

Since the barrel dips too far down as the barrel approaches the plane of the pitch, **the hands over-correct by rolling over, which causes the ground-balls.**

The problem with these hitters is the hands aren't connected to the turning torso.

And this is where Finger Pressure comes in.

TWO Case Studies

Jace was a 10yo hitter who weighed 60 pounds when I first started working with him (image above).

His initial Ball-Exit-Speed readings were all over the map, topping out at 46-mph with a metal bat.

He had racing back elbow bat drag BAD.

Dad told me, **his coach would ask him to bunt most of his at-bats during the game because he couldn't get the ball out of the infield**.

He's above average at bunting by the way, and he's fast.

I wasn't aware of Finger Pressure for the first 4-5 months working with him, and we tried EVERYTHING to fix his racing back elbow.

Nothing seemed to work.

Enter Finger Pressure.

At about month 6, we started working on Jace's Finger Pressure...

After two-weeks, two sessions total in that span, he was executing the technique we're about to describe in 80% of his swings.

His Ball-Exit-Speed after that time jumped to a 55-mph high, and a tighter average scatter range between 50-54-mph.

Racing back elbow was gone at the end of 2-weeks. As long as he was using Finger Pressure like he was supposed to.

He hit his first 180-foot home-run at 11yo, which cleared the fence by 20-feet, weighing in at 67-pounds.

NOTE: The extra 7-pounds were gained by adding one big Costco chocolate muffin to his breakfast every morning!

I started working with Zack when he was an 8th grader. His frame was tall and slender, about 6'4", 155-pounds. He was going into High School with coaches talking about him as a "pitcher-only".

Zack also had racing back elbow bad, and we tried for 2 years to kick the habit. We tried everything.

His initial Ball-Exit-Speed readings were scattered with a high of about 77-mph.

Enter Finger Pressure.

The day I introduced his swing to Finger Pressure, it took only one 30-minute session. His racing back elbow disappeared.

His Ball-Exit-Speeds stabilized, moving between 79 and 83-mph. He was hitting balls in games like he had never thought possible.

The tragic story with Zack was that the coaches had already made up their minds to make him a pitcher-only.

We spent 2.5 years working together.

Here are the observational benefits I've found with Finger Pressure…

This is Zack in the one 30-min session we stopped his racing back elbow bat drag.

> 1. Connects hands and bat to the turning torso via Anatomical Trains of fascia,
> 2. **Stabilizes erratic Ball Exit Speeds**,
> 3. Boosts Ball Exit Speeds dramatically,
> 4. Enables hitter to hit bat's sweet spot more often, and
> 5. **Busts racing back elbow bat drag in a relatively short amount of time**.

You can see their story and an updated Finger-Pressure-Experiment at the following link:
http://gohpl.com/fingerpressureexperiment
The technique is this…

THE HOW-to of Finger Pressure

Top hand ONLY, squeezing hard the bottom three fingers…including the pinky, ring, and middle fingers. This would be the right hand for a righty, left hand for a lefty.

On a scale of one to ten, a TEN being crushing charcoal into a diamond...I want my hitters squeezing at least an 8.

The bottom hand uses what I call "butterfly grip" pressure...

The hitter's bottom hand holds the handle of the bat like they would a butterfly they don't want to crush or let go free.

Finger Pressure is turned on and off like a light switch...

It's turned on when the hitter picks up the stride foot – or starts the swing – and turned off well past impact.

The bottom hand is focused on butterfly grip pressure for just as long.

The hitter can use Finger Pressure on the bottom hand, but isn't necessary.

I spoke of how well bottom-hand butterfly-grip pressure worked for me the summer before my Junior season in High School.

Top hand, bottom three fingers squeezed ONLY.

I don't advise my hitters to create bottom-hand tension anymore because there are hitters out there using too much of the

Not too tight to kill the butterfly, and not too loose to let him go.

bottom hand and arm to swing the bat.

Primarily, crossed-up hitters...those right handed batters, but left handed throwers (and vice-versa), because this places their dominant hand on bottom.

We have to educate the top hand for these hitters, which can take a little longer in reaching the objective.

7

CHAPTER 7

*"There is a huge amount of this connective tissue that can make your golf swing more powerful, if you choose to use it (**locking your spine in a stiff, straight line is a way of not using it**)."*
– Kelvin Miyahira

The "Hunched" Posture

Primarily focusing on "hip thrust", which can exaggerate the turning of the pelvis to initiate the turn of the swing, **can really move the lower back of hitters into dangerous waters, if repeated over and over for thousands of repetitions**.

WHY?

Because EVERY movement, for ANY athlete, MUST be initiated by the spine in total, not just one piece of it…and in the hip-thrust case, the lower-back.

You'll learn how to safely "pre-load" the swing using the shoulders in CHAPTER 8.

But for now…

Let me ask you this…

If you were to swing a sledge hammer or a long-handled axe into a cinder block wall or tree trunk…

Would you thrust your hips at the target, and hope and pray your shoulders just slingshot around?

How long do you think you can keep that up before developing (*according to OrthoInfo.aaos.org*):

- **Spondylolysis** (a fracturing of the vertebrae)? OR over time and many thousands of reps later…
- **Spondylolisthesis**, more severe, which is where the fractured vertebra slips out of place and may begin to press on nearby nerves. Spondylolisthesis can cause back spasms, tightening both the back and hamstring muscles…

This is where the information in this book diverges away from conventional hitting philosophy.

Most experts out there are too married to their "hip-thrust" hitting philosophy; they miss what's really important to young developing hitters.

SAFETY.

The good news is…

Your hitters won't sacrifice power for safety in using the Hunched Posture.

There has got to be…

A Better Way

"If you were to sit on a ball bucket and play video games for an hour, what shape would your spine take during that time?"

This is a question I ask my hitters when instructing on the shape their spine should take pre-turn.

I tell my hitters that you get a get-out-of-jail-free-card to hunch while hitting, whereas most get a stern "sit up straight" order at the dinner table.

Do you know why we all default back to this hunched posture for long periods of sitting time?

The answer is, it allows the vertebrae in our spine to decompress.

We'll come back to this…

But first I want to address,

Why we don't want our hitters striving for a neutral spine, or straight-back in the stance.

Coach Sommers, the former Men's Olympic Gymnastics coach and founder of GymnasticBodies.com, in a Tim Ferriss podcast, **said explosive movement isn't ALL about getting and maintaining a neutral spine.**

He notes his Gymnasts move from Global Extension and Flexion of the spine during competition and practice. Neutral spinal positions are just a pass-through. This is how flips can be so explosive.

If you're late to the party, and don't know what "neutral spine" means, then let's answer the question of how to get into one…

Stand with your feet under your shoulders, toes straight ahead, and arms hanging by your sides…

Squeeze your butt cheeks together as tight as possible, this will put your pelvis and low back in neutral.

Now, with your butt cheeks squeezed, tighten your abdominals as tight as you can, this will most likely pull your rib cage down. This will put the 'L' and 'T' spine connection in neutral…

And lastly, while doing both of the above, take your shoulders and roll them up, back, and down, and this will put the totality of the 'T' spine in neutral.

CONGRATS!!

Now you have neutral spine…

I now challenge you to slowly release the muscle tension and hold the positions we put your pelvis, spine, and shoulders into.

Let's get back to the Hunched Posture,

Now, sitting hunched on the bucket while playing, *Tour of Duty*, notice what state the abdominals are in?

Are they contracted?

They may not be contracted like you were during the Neutral Spine exercise, but they are to some degree.

You see, as I described earlier in the book, the lower back is naturally in an extended position called lordosis…remember the 'C' shape?

When you're in the hunched position, we call it taking the curve out of the 'C'.

For those of you who've been to a Physical Therapist because of lower-back issues, **what's one of the first exercises they have you do?**

Most likely, it's lying on your back, in a "crunch-ready" position with knees up and feet flat on the ground...

Then, they'll ask you to push your lower-back into the ground for a certain amount of time, or do say 15-20 reps of this over 4-5 sets.

What I learned from second to none strength and conditioning coach, Paul Chek, is to slightly inflate a blood pressure cuff to about 40 mm's of Mercury, place this under the lower-back arch while the client is relaxed (typically directly below the belly button). Then, **have them push their lower- back into the cuff, and hold the needle at 70 mm's of Mercury.**

You can make the exercise harder by having the client pick up their feet and maintain control over the needle...OR, taking this one step further, have them move their legs away from them and back, while maintaining control over the needle.

Once the client cannot control the needle any longer – hint – the needle begins dancing all over the place, they must rest.

If you really want a challenge, try the Gymnastics' Hollow-Hold Position, while using the blood pressure cuff.

What does this little exercise do?

A couple things:

- **Allows for better pelvic control**, going from anterior to posterior pelvic tilt (think Pink Panther v. Donald Duck, respectively),
- **Takes pressure off vertebrae** in Lower Back because of decompression,
- **Strengthens the abdominals and psoas** to keep the Lumbar SAFE and stable, and
- **Allows you to pick up heavy objects** without hurting your low back!

Directed at the last point...

Really!?

There's power in taking the curve out of the lower back 'C'?

Yes.

In Dr. Serge Gracovetsky's book, *The Spinal Engine*, he shared a study where he had normal people doing a dead lift.

In this experiment, Professor Gracovetsky monitored key muscles and Posterior-Ligament-Tissue-activation. The latter he calls the Posterior Ligament System, or PLS, which **acts like a harness to the lower-back, butt, and legs...similar to a harness you'd wear while rock climbing.**

I can't remember the actual breaking point, but it was something like when people lifting less than 150-pounds, they preserved the ability to "keep their back straight", which is a conventional coaching cue for this particular lift.

The Professor showed a dramatic increase in muscle activation here, with minimal PLS activation.

However, **once the weight approached and surpassed the 150-pound threshold, we saw the back round (Globally Flex), muscles deactivate, and PLS dramatically activate.**

Now, from the ground, you don't want to go around dead-lifting heavy objects starting with a rounded back. You still have to take 'slack' out of the system by loading the hamstrings, butt, and lats first.

You see,

The PLS system acts as a safety harness after the weight has been lifted off the ground, to get to the final standing position.

And if you don't believe me:

1. Read Dr. Serge Gracovetsky's book, AND
2. Pull up the YouTube video, "2014 Arnold Strongman Zydrunas Savickas deadlift 1155 pounds" – and observe if he's keeping his back straight the entire lift.

What's more…?

While we're here, let's discuss,

Taking slack out of the system

It's an important point that's worth noting…

Example number one,

Think of a car that's fallen into a shallow ravine. You've pulled up to the top of the ravine to help your friend. Attached to the front bumper of your Jeep Wrangler is a wench.

You take the wench hook, stumble down the short ravine slanted dirt wall, and attach it to the bumper of your friend's car. Since you've never used this feature before, you leave slack in the cable that connects the hook to the wench motor unit.

You climb back to the top of the ravine and turn the wench on…but it pulls your friend's bumper off!

What did you do wrong?

You left slack in the cable dummy! lol

Repeat everything in scenario #1, but instead of turning the wench on and 'letting 'er fly', slowly pull the cable slack out, then 'let 'er fly'…like magic your friend now owes you a couple rounds of Lagunitas IPA beer.

That's my favorite by the way, in case you were wondering.

Example number two,

Imagine a train engine, carrying about 25 boxcars behind it. The engine starts up and begins pulling the boxcars.

Question…

Does the whole train begin moving forward right away?

Most likely, not.

Why?

Because all the slack MUST be taken out of the connectors between the boxcars first. Plain Physics. Heavy things at rest tend to stay at rest until acted upon by a bigger force.

The loud "clanging" sound one hears, precedes the train making forward progress.

Once all the slack is taken out, the train moves forward.

Loading the body looks slightly different, because we're talking about the compression tension forces discussed back in CHAPTER 5.

Don't worry, we'll get into how this applies to hitting in CHAPTERS 8 & 9.

Okay, so you understand the benefits to the hunched posture, and taking slack out of the system, but still aren't clear how this applies to baseball and softball hitters…

Here's a Quick Way to Fix the Dreaded "C-Shape Impact" Position...

What is the 'C-Shape' impact position?

For righties, the 'C-Shape' is reversed...for lefties, the 'C-Shape' is conventional.

The 'C-Shape' forms at and post impact. **The head drifts over the catcher, taking the rib cage with it.** So, if you draw a curved line tracing the head, back, and back leg, you'll see a 'C-Shape'.

If you look at the left panel image of 11-year-old, softball-hitter, Lauryn above, her abdominals are stretching, which indicates the lower-back could possibly be in hyper-extension...not good.

This is not adhering to the One-Joint Rule discuss we discuss in CHAPTER 11.

11yo Lauryn BEFORE & AFTER activating the Hunched Posture. Photo courtesy: Dad

The two problems with 'C-Shape' Impact are:

- **Bleeding force at impact**, and
- **UNSAFE for low back**.

The answer can be found in what Gymnasts refer to as, the Hollow-Hold Position.

Search on YouTube: "how to do a hollow hold: gymnastics" for a video on this.

Here was the corrective programming homework I gave Lauryn who's one of my online lessons:

- **Week one:** 1 set X 20-30 secs hold,
- **Week two:** 1 set X 30-40 secs hold,
- **Week three:** 2 sets X 30 secs hold, and
- **Week four:** 2 sets X 45 secs hold

...Do every other day.

The keys with this move is constantly applying pressure into the ground with the low back, and rounding the shoulders forward to create a 'spoon' or 'hollow' position with the chest.

This helps with pelvic control (rotating the pelvis to posterior), stabilizes the low back, and is KILLER for the abs – in a good way.

Notice this is the same spinal position you'd take if you had to sit on a bucket for four-hours playing video games.

Young athletes know this position well, but **most likely haven't applied it to their hitting stance**.

The fix that helped Lauryn fix the 'C-Shape' impact position in less than 24-hours was the Hunched Posture...

So, how do we get our hitters in the Hunched Position?

Sorry to do this to you again, but...

Before discussing how to get hitters into this position,

I want to appeal to those who LOVE analyzing the best hitters with slow-motion video...

Go look at the following hitters, and note which shape their spine starts in – let me give you a clue – you're looking for a well-rounded back, or a Globally Flexed spine (this list is non-exhaustive):

- Hunter Pence,
- Ben Zobrist (especially from the left side),
- Josh Donaldson,
- Sadaharu Oh,
- Ted Williams,
- Mel Ott,
- Pete Rose,
- Ty Cobb,
- Babe Ruth, and
- Mickey Mantle (especially from the left side)...

Seek and you will most surely find.

A good reference point to use for your search, would be to compare to Derek Jeter, who's back was a straight as an arrow when hitting.

The Hunched Posture drill steps go like this...

1. Sit on ball bucket like you were to play video games for 4 hours,
2. Now grab your bat and act like you're going to hit, still keeping the hunched posture,
3. Keeping the rounded back, now stand up and apply that position to your normal stance.

Hitters that are used to the "straight back" when hitting, will find it hard to maintain the Hunched Posture when standing up in their batting stance.

Keep sitting them down, repeating the steps, and standing them back up until they get it – with your feedback of course.

Once they get it, they won't let go of it. My hitters report back their feelings that the Hunched Posture:

My 13yo hitter Mikey hunching his middle back.

- *"Just feels better",*
- *"Helps show numbers and downhill shoulder angle",* and most importantly,
- *"My back feels nothing while swinging"* (a good thing! lol).

See CHAPTER 12 on how to infuse mechanical variations to help them get this lesson faster during actual swings.

At the close of this CHAPTER, I wanted leave you with a Zepp-swing-experiment, where I tested this...

I did a Hunch v. NO Hunch swing experiment, and the most interesting thing I observed was that **I increased my barrel's Attack Angle by 4-degrees (positive) by using Hunched posture**.

That's HUGE!

We want the barrel coming up (positive angle) to meet the downward traveling ball, not down (negative) to meet it.

The other thing I observed in the experiment was that Bat Speed at Impact and Hand Speed Max DID NOT change.

Therefore, like I said earlier, **your hitters won't sacrifice power for safety in using the Hunched Posture...PLUS, they'll gain some positive barrel Attack Angle points!**

You can view the swing experiment at the following url: http://gohpl.com/hunchedposture

Mikey with his back straight.

8

CHAPTER 8

"You can avoid reality, but you cannot avoid the consequences of avoiding reality."
– Ayn Rand

To Show the Numbers, or NOT to Show the Numbers…that is the Question

In February of 2015, I started advertising on Facebook.

For an email address, I gave coaches a 10-minute video with the following title:

"NEW Zepp Swing Study Reveals #1 Dead Simple Strategy That Added 24-48 Feet To Batted Ball Distance (HINT: and it's Not ALL in the Hips)…"

Some of you may have seen it already.

Do you know how many times that video was downloaded?

Over 12,000 times!!

Over 4,000 times within the first 3-weeks alone!!

The first-third of the video showcased one of the first few swing-experiments I did, using the Zepp app.

I did 100 swings 'showing pitcher my numbers' and another 100 swings 'NOT showing pitcher my numbers' at landing.

Here's the link to the original experiment blog post video:

http://gohpl.com/shownumbersexperiment

Here are a couple observations found…

I averaged 6-mph more Bat Speed at Impact 'showing my numbers' than 'NOT showing my numbers.

In addition, **I averaged 2-mph more Hand Speed Max, 'showing numbers'** versus NOT.

I know, I know…

Some of you will say "Who cares about Bat Speed. What's the gain in Ball-Exit-Speed (or BES)?"

I'll get there, but first it may be interesting for you to note that retired Professor Emeritus of Physics at the University of Illinois at Urbana-Champaign, Dr. Alan Nathan, says the biggest effect on BES is…wait for it…Bat Speed!

If Bat Speed is low, then so will Ball-Exit-Speed.

I do have a treat for those obsessed with BES though…

Hot off the press, I finished another 'show numbers' versus 'NOT show numbers' experiment capturing Ball Exit Speed, and the results were more dramatic than I thought…

- Average BES when '**showing numbers**' was 74.65-mph
- Average BES when '**NOT showing numbers**' was 65.04-mph

Do the math!!

Just kidding, I'm not going to make you do the math. lol

That's a **9.61-mph difference**!!

What does that mean in relation to batted-ball distance?

I'm conservative with my translation of BES/batted ball distance…every 1-mph of BES equals 4-feet of distance.

So multiplying the above 9.61-mph BES difference by 4-feet of distance, that's an **EXTRA 38.44-feet of distance just by** 'showing the pitcher your numbers'!!

Do I have your attention yet?

This is where it's at folks!

Before I get into the nuts and bolts of the technique, I want to flesh out some of the objections to 'showing the numbers' other coaches raise…

Shifts impact point towards catcher thereby increasing Time to Impact

First of all, go onto MLB.com, and sort offensive stats by high OPS (On-base Plus Slugging)…

Take the top 20-30 hitters and filter out the small sluggers from the big ones, using our criteria of small sluggers being 6-foot on down, weighing less than 215-pounds or so.

Now, go to YouTube and search "[name of small slugger] 2016 highlights".

Here comes the punch line…now, **observe how many small sluggers 'show their numbers' just before landing**.

'NOT showing numbers' is just NOT what we're seeing on video with small sluggers…and if you want to take it one step farther, look at vintage power sluggers. A large majority are 'showing the numbers'.

'Showing numbers' does not shift the impact point towards the catcher, **unless the hitter is taught to inwardly turn the hips (actually the pelvis) towards the catcher** during the load.

This actually dampens the effect of 'showing numbers', because if you remember the Springy 'X' Pattern discussed earlier, it doesn't allow the shortening of the front shoulder to back hip leg of the 'X' on the chest.

The pelvis MUST remain in neutral, or parallel to the plate, to landing.

We'll go into the mechanics in more detail later, but you need to know, **it's the hips that set the impact point, not the shoulders**.

And about Time To Impact, this just isn't true.

Number one,

Go back and read about 'taking slack out of the system' I mentioned earlier. With the human body, we're doing this by pre-loading the torso before unwinding the body into the ball.

And number two,

In the most recent counter-balanced 'Showing Numbers' experiment, I actually **showed Time to Impact decreasing by .003 seconds** when the hitter "shows their numbers".

The original 'Showing Numbers' experiment showed a .003 second increase in Time To Impact when 'showing numbers', however that experiment wasn't counter-balanced.

Won't the hitter lose sight of the ball by showing pitcher their numbers?

I have my hitters use what I call the "back eye" test...

My hitter gets to the landing position, which I call the "Fight" position, showing their numbers.

I stand out front of the hitter, in the pitched ball line of sight, and instruct them to close their front eye.

With the front eye closed (left eye for a righty), I then ask them if they can see me with their back eye (right eye for a righty).

If they cannot, then they're showing the numbers too much. If it's too easy, then I tell them to "show me more numbers" until they get close to not being able to see me with the back eye.

We use what I call the Goldilocks-Golden-Rule...don't pick the porridge that's too hot or too cold...pick the one that's just right.

The same goes for showing the numbers, or any hitting mechanism we talk about in this book for that matter. **Find out what *feels* right for the hitter, but still accomplishes the mechanical objective.**

You're teaching to hit with the shoulders, I thought the hips lead the way?

Yes, and yes...generally speaking.

Specifically speaking however, **I'm teaching my hitters to hit with the WHOLE Spinal Engine**, not with one piece over another...

That's the difference, which is HUGE, because most teach with a "hips only" approach, forgetting the shoulders altogether.

Yes, the hips do lead the way – for a right-handed hitter, **the pelvis is the first piece of the Engine to start turning counter-clockwise.**

This is because as the stride foot approaches the ground, the pelvis may start to open...this depends on timing and pitch type.

According to Dr. Serge Gracovetsky,

As the front foot and leg receive the body's weight, a compression signal from the ground, thanks to Gravitational Reaction Forces, shoots up the front leg hitting the pelvis, signaling them to turn counter-clockwise...again, we're speaking of a right-handed hitter.

That **same compression signal continues up the spine into the shoulders, signaling the shoulders to make a counter move**...to turn clockwise...

However,

We've already pre-loaded the shoulders' pre-landing by 'Showing Numbers', so because we've 'taken out the slack', the shoulders can begin their counter-clockwise move into impact.

You see, **our pelvis and shoulders move counter to each other, like a gear shift**. Or how we twist off a bottle cap...this is what "torque" is, in a nutshell.

Again, this is why our right arm and left leg swing forward at the same time when walking.

Coaches, it's ineffective to tell hitters to:

- 'Load and explode the hips'
- Make 'the hips lead the way', or
- 'Thrust those hips into the ball!'

Since I started teaching this material, I've NEVER mentioned the hips – or pelvis – to my hitters once, in this sense.

I don't have to.

For most right-handed hitters, the pelvis will automatically start their counter-clockwise rotation at landing, and clockwise, for a lefty.

It's what the hitter does before landing, or near landing, that matters.

Let me give you a clue – it's not ALL about the hips. In my opinion, the hips and the rotation of them are over taught.

How do we teach 'showing the numbers', so hitters can benefit from that extra 38-feet of batted ball distance?

The good news is…

Most of the heavy lifting has been done already…

> 1. **Making sure the hitter is 'showing their numbers' to the pitcher, as close to landing as possible**, and
> 2. Use the "Back Eye" Test to make sure they're not showing too much…

I wanted to add a couple more important points.

Number one,

It's challenging for hitters to know if they're 'showing numbers' or 'NOT showing numbers' if they practice putting their swing together at first.

What I mean by that is,

I do what's called the Break It Apart Drill, which actually isn't a drill, but more about breaking the swing down into two parts:

> 1. Getting to the Fight Position (landing),
> 2. Pausing 1-2 seconds, and then
> 3. Doing the Final Turn (swinging the bat).

My 13yo hitter 'Showing the Numbers'

This gives the body a chance to catch up with the brain.

In the last Chapter of this book, we'll go over progressing and regressing drills for the stickiest effect on learning.

But for now, I just want you to note that this is **where I start my hitters when working on a brand spanking new motor skill**.

Point number two,

And this is a biggie…

At the landing position, **the pelvis MUST be running parallel to home plate, so in order to achieve this, we do what I call the Flashlight Front Knee Drill**.

In this drill, I want the hitter's landing knee to be pointing at the second baseman, for a righty, and at the shortstop, for a lefty.

This ensures the pelvis stays in a neutral position and does not close off the front side.

Hitter 'NOT Showing the Numbers'

The combination of 'Showing Numbers' and shining landing knee flashlight at the opposite field middle infielder; **we get the maximum effect of springy fascia**.

9

CHAPTER 9

"Enjoy your sweat because hard work doesn't guarantee success, but without it, you don't have a chance."
– Alex Rodriguez

Down Gets It Done!

To kick off this CHAPTER, I wanted to share this testimonial with you…

It's from a Florida father, talking about his – at the time – 13yo fast-pitch softball daughter, who I trained in my online video hitting lessons program *The Feedback Lab*:

"Hey Coach,

It has been way too long but I wanted to share some information that happened yesterday. We are heading up to Chattanooga, Tennessee, the largest showcase in the southeast today. Yesterday was our last day to hit before the showcase and **Mia was struggling with her power**. *We hit about 60-70 balls and Mia was hitting about 10% over the fence (she is usually 40%+). I was looking to make sure she was showing her number, which she was, hiding her hands, which she was, landing with a bent knee, which she was and etc., etc. It was getting late and we had to go and I told Mia she had only 6 balls left. I told her to show me her stance and I noticed that her front shoulder was equal to her back shoulder. I then told her to lower her front shoulder and raise her back one. That was the only change we made to her swing, Mia then hit the next 6 balls over the fence and 2 of them were bombs.* **I cannot believe the difference this one small change made.**

Thanks,

Primo"

Let me just say, before giving any instruction to Mia, she was doing well. *The Catapult Loading System* just amplified what she already had going for her. And by the way, she's a SUPER hard worker.

I can't stress the following enough…

How well this system works for BOTH baseball and softball hitters.

NOT 7 year-olds versus 24 year-olds…NOT boys versus girls…NOT big versus small bodies…and NOT elite hitters versus amateurs.

We're talking humans here.

A word of caution coaches, before we dig into the role of the shoulders in the swing,

Make sure you keep the Goldilocks Golden Rule in mind…

Again, we can do it too much, or like in most cases, not at all.

One of the following Zepp-swing-experiments I did was testing the effect of Downhill Shoulders as close to landing as possible versus keeping the shoulders level as close to landing as possible.

The post analyzed one of the best hitters at using, *The Catapult Loading System*, Downhill Shoulders specifically, **Miguel Cabrera, whose shoulders get to about an 8-degree down-angle pre-landing**.

The title of the post was, *"Baseball Swing Load: If You Can Bend Sideways You Can Gain 4-MPH Bat Speed"*.

Here's a link to this swing-experiment:

http://gohpl.com/downshouldersexperiment

The two big benefits I observed when comparing the Zepp metrics were a:

- **4-mph average increase in Bat Speed at Impact with Downhill Shoulders** versus level shoulders at landing, and
- **3-degree increase in a positive-barrel-Attack-Angle with Downhill Shoulders** versus level shoulders at landing.
- **BONUS: Time To Impact decrease** of an average of .003 seconds with Downhill Shoulders

I take some of my hitters through a visual exercise, where I have them pretend to be standing on top of a small hill, and the pitcher is pitching to them from the bottom, and that's where the coaching cue 'Down Shoulders' was born.

Now, I know you're asking yourself these questions...

Why? What's going on here?

This goes back to Dr. Serge Gracovetsky's *The Spinal Engine*.

Remember the three possible spinal movements referenced by the Physics and Electical-Engineering Professor...?

1. **Extension/Flexion** (arching, a la Upward Facing Dog Pose OR crunching, a la Hollow Position)
2. **Lateral Flexion** (aka side bending)
3. **Axial Rotation** (shoulders moving opposite pelvis)

Here's a clue – Lordosis in the lower-back (#1) is already present, or if the hitter starts in the Hunched Posture, which I recommended in CHAPTER 7, then we've checked Flexion (#1) off our list instead.

'Showing Numbers' allows us to pre-load the torso and take slack out of the system (#3), **but it's Side-Bending (#2, aka Downhill Shoulders) that really initiates explosive Axial Rotation (#3) into impact**.

I mentioned this observation in CHAPTER 5 of this book, but it's worth circling back to illustrate the point...

What we should see in a safe and effective Spinal Engine is:

1. The shoulders start in a downhill angle, as close to landing as possible (between six to ten-degrees *down* gets it done),
2. As the turn starts, the shoulders will flip, for instance, a right-handed hitter's right shoulder will start up, then at the beginning of the turn, it flips down, and THEN

3. During the hitter's follow-through, we will see the shoulder angle flip back to how it started with the right shoulder up, but twisted around.

Think about the beautiful finishes of Ted Williams, Mickey Mantle, and Lou Gehrig.

Now, let me be clear here...

When the hitter begins weighting their front leg, the shoulders will be about *level*, not down.

However, **I coach my hitters to hold the shoulders down to 'as close to landing as possible'.**

The hitters that have the biggest challenge with this, are ones angling the shoulders up when the weight shift releases to the front leg, and most likely are over-rotating their upper torso too soon.

Now, let's discuss coaching out of extremes...

Coaches BEWARE!!

The American way of, if a little is good, then A LOT will be better...DOES NOT apply here.

Hitters will test motor skill extremes, and sometimes they'll stick.

For example,

One of my hitters, 13-year-old, Mikey, who I've worked with since he was 7-years-old...

In his last tournament, on a Little League diamond in Cooperstown,

Out of 12 games, he hit 9 homers, 4 were Grand Slams, and one of the dingers traveled well over 270-feet!

Oh, and he didn't just hit homers, his batting average was something like .700 for the tourney.

It didn't matter if a pitcher with above average or below average stuff came in, he CRUSHED.

He did well this season, with many multi-homer games and near cycles, but never put together an insane offensive output like that.

So, what led up to that week?

That **whole season was a challenge for him timing-wise.**

You see, he's younger for his age, and attends a K-8 school, so he started the year hitting off 60-foot mounds...

Then switched to Pony Rule 50-foot mounds...

Then switched back to Little league 46-foot mounds...

We do train this variance in the cage, but I'm not sure how much he did on his own time.

Long story short,

We did two things...

Number one,

We did a two-plate drill that you'll learn in the last CHAPTER called the **Varied Reaction LIVE-Toss-Timing-Drill that calibrates a hitter's timing.**

I made this drill so challenging for him 3-4 weeks leading up to the Cooperstown tournament.

And number two,

We had to scale down his shoulder angle (pardon the pun).

In other words, he had too much of a Downhill Shoulder angle, **resulting in an extreme uppercut and hole in his swing with pitches up in the zone.**

He was venturing into the 14-degree plus territory!

...Like a golfer, which is fine, because they don't have to hit golf balls above their knees.

So, how did we scale down Mikey's extreme shoulder angle?

The following coaching cue works, whether we're talking an extreme down-shoulder-angle like Mikey's, level shoulders, or sometimes, even up like so many young hitters nowadays.

We use the back elbow as a brain reference point to adjust the shoulder angle.

Wa??!

Why not manipulate the shoulders!?

For some reason in the past, when I've tried coaching the shoulders and not the back elbow, **the message occasionally got lost in translation and the mechanical changes were inconsistent for Downhill Shoulders**.

An example of this was, I would tell my hitter to 'tuck the front shoulder inside the front hip' before landing, and with some hitters it would work, but with most, it wouldn't. Some new hitting flaw would pop up.

I've heard other coaches, like Primo Buffano, in the testimonial at the beginning of this CHAPTER, say, *"lower your front shoulder and raise the back one",* and *"lower your front armpit and raise the back one."*

My 13yo Hitter Mikey with his "Healthy" Downhill Shoulder Angle

Anyway, I've had minimal challenges with coaching the back elbow.

So, as a general rule, I cue my hitters to get their back elbow up to either level with the top hand or slightly above it, as close to landing as possible.

And this will depend on where the hitter naturally gets their hands to at landing, and just before the turn initiates.

For instance, if the hitter lands with hands held higher, then you don't want to coach them to get the back elbow higher...

WHY?

Because now they'll have an extreme down-shoulder-angle.

So, what I'd do in this instance, is lower the hands in the stance, and get them to move the top hand to not much higher than the back shoulder before landing. I wouldn't allow their hands to get above the armpit level to landing, and this makes it easier to raise the back elbow and create that downhill angle with the shoulders.

That way, once we move the back elbow up, the down shoulder angle falls within our 6-10 degrees down range.

Now, let's talk about the second to last component of *The Catapult Loading System...*

Mikey with Level Shoulders

10

CHAPTER 10

*"Do not seek to follow in the footsteps of others, instead, **seek what they sought.**"*
– Matsuo Basho

Hiding the Hands from the Pitcher

Some may call this the 'Scap Row', shortened for "Scapular Row". Google "scap row baseball swing", and I'm sure you'll get plenty coming up about it.

What you'll see from the pitcher's viewpoint is the back elbow peeking out from behind the hitter's backside close to landing.

I have a beef with using the words "Scap Row" as a coaching cue...
WHY?

Because how many average Joe's know what that means??!

There's so much confusion on the net surrounding this one coaching cue. I know because I get questions emailed to me weekly about it. What is it? How does it work? Blah, blah, blah.

Here's a clue...

Coaching cues are most effective when you can say them to someone who's never worked with you before, and they do exactly what you're telling them to do.

'Hide your hands from the pitcher' is a coaching cue my 4-year-old understands.

My 13yo hitter 'Hiding the Hands'

Here's where I'm going to upset some people fully invested in the 'Scap Row' as the end-all-be-all to power...

I'm not fully convinced the 'Scap Row', done in isolation (without 'showing numbers'), dramatically improves power.

For the budding swing-experimenters out there, here are a couple ideas to test...

Hitter 'NOT Hiding the Hands'. Note absence of the back elbow peaking out.

- Keeping front shoulder pointing straight ahead at landing, what's the difference in Bat or Ball-Exit-Speed with splitting 200 counter-balanced swings between a 'Scap Row' versus 'NO Scap Row'? Or, how about...
- While 'Showing Numbers' at landing, what is the difference in Bat or Ball-Exit-Speed with splitting 200 counter-balanced swings between a 'Scap Row' (or 'Hiding the Hands') versus 'NOT Hiding the Hands'?

Well, guess what, we have an app...ahem...I mean an experiment for that!

In July of 2015, I had a college baseball player intern for me named Tyler Doerner.
One of the Zepp experiments he did, helped shed light on the second bullet point above...
Here's what came out of the data analysis:

- On average, a **1-mph increase in average-Bat-Speed at Impact** by 'Hiding Hands' versus NOT,
- On average, a **1-mph increase in average-Hand-Speed-Max** by 'Hiding Hands' versus NOT, and
- On average, a **.005 decrease in Time-To-Impact** by 'Hiding Hands' versus NOT.

What's also interesting to note, there was a difference in top-out bat speeds:

- Top-4 'Hiding the Hands' Bat Speeds (in mph): 85, 84, 84, and 82.
- Top-4 'Not Hiding the Hands' Bat Speeds (in mph): 82, 81, and the rest were less than 79.

So, there was a slight change in performance with 'Hiding the Hands', aka 'Scap Row', rather than not doing it, **but is it a dramatic increase in power versus 'Showing the Numbers'?**
No.
WHY?
Because 'Showing Numbers' is at the heart of Dr. Serge Gracovetsky's, *The Spinal Engine*.
There is a benefit however...

"Hiding Hands" optimizes Springy 'X' Pattern

Let's circle back to the imaginary 'X' on your chest and back, that we looked into in CHAPTER 5, where one shoulder is connected to the opposite hip, thanks to the network of springy fascia...

Remember, to maximize springy forces for the chest or back, one leg of the 'X' MUST get shorter, while the other leg of the 'X' MUST get longer.

If 'Showing Numbers' and 'Downhill Shoulders' help bring the front shoulder closer to the back hip, then **what aids the back shoulder to move away from the front hip?**

That's right!

'Hiding the Hands'.

Putting it all Together

We're not done yet.

We have one more human-movement-principle to go over, but I'd be remiss if I didn't tie the following together because I know you still have logistical questions...

I like to call the last few principles we went over the BIG-3:

1. **Showing Numbers,**
2. **Downhill Shoulders,** and
3. **Hiding the Hands.**

So, you've stuck with me this far...

You've seen the competitive advantages the above three principles give a hitter in isolation...

The next logical question a coach would ask is...

Do you teach these separately or as one movement piece?

Yes, and yes.

I'd teach them separately at first, then once the hitter gains motor skill mastery, I'd teach them to use these movements as one fluid motion.

The next question I get asked is, so when does the load start?

And my answer is...

It depends.

It depends on what the hitter is comfortable with.

What's great about these three springy fascia principles, is **the hitter can start them in their stance.**

You see,

It doesn't matter whether a hitter starts in them or moves into them, the springy effect is virtually the same.

I recommend to my younger hitters to start in the Catapult Loaded position.

In other words, in the hitter's stance, they're 'Showing Numbers', have 'Downhill Shoulders', and are 'Hiding Hands'...

And they will hold that position until they get to stride landing. DO NOT start in the Catapult Loading Position, then move deeper into it during the stride and landing. Remember what I said about the Goldilocks Golden Rule? Too much...not doing it at all...we want the position just right.

A couple MLB hitter examples that tend to start in this position are:

- Hunter Pence,
- Ben Zobrist (from the left side),
- Yoenis Cespedes, and
- Stan Musial.

A majority of hitters however, move into the Catapult Loaded Position as they're picking up their front foot to start their Float and Fall, or "Ride and Stride" (thanks Matt Nokes!!).

A couple of MLB hitter examples that tend to move into this position are:

- Ted Williams,

- Dustin Pedroia,
- Sadaharu Oh, and
- Robinson Cano.

I'm sorry coaches, if you think that a hitter loads by inwardly turning the hips towards the catcher, in addition to doing a 'Scap Row'...**this isn't optimized loading, and your hitters are leaving consistent power on the table.**

Let's move onto the last human-movement-principle that's validated by science in *The Catapult Loading System...*

11

CHAPTER 11

"An investment in knowledge pays the best interest."
– Benjamin Franklin

Head Position: The One-Joint Rule

It's funny…

Self-proclaimed hitting enthusiasts on social media get so upset when it's mentioned that one of their beloved elite hitters has a chink in their mechanical armor…

Some get their panties in a bunch when we point out those hitters such as Andrew McCutchen, Bryce Harper, Prince Fielder, Nolan Arenado, and Derek Jeter actually have flaws in their swing.

This is where, looking to human-movement-principles first, then video analysis second, works its magic.

We have to understand some elite hitters succeed despite ineffective mechanics, NOT because of them.

We'll discuss the flaw in these hitters shortly, but first I want to jump into the application because I think it'll give context to the subject of head position and how some of the best, as cross-fit Physical Therapist. Dr. Kelly Starrett says, are "bleeding force" at impact.

I use the One-Joint Rule Test with my hitters…

Borrowed from Dr. Kelly Starrett **to explain to them the power of head position at impact**, in his book, *"Becoming a Supple Leopard 2nd Edition: The Ultimate Guide to Resolving Pain, Preventing Injury, and Optimizing Athletic Performance"*…

The following link is a video of me demonstrating his One-Joint Rule Test with one of my past athletes:

http://gohpl.com/onejointruletest

I'll walk you through it in the following…

This takes two people,

Imagine the athlete standing tall with feet positioned under shoulders, arms at their sides, and staring straight ahead.

Now, instruct the athlete to raise a straight dominant arm in front of them with the hand about shoulder height. I will use the right arm raised for this example. For those gym rats that understand, basically **a front shoulder raise with a neutral hand position, or palm facing body's center line.**

Instruct the athlete to "splay" their right hand's fingers wide (this gives a cue to the right elbow to tighten)…

Then tell the athlete, **you're going to attempt to bend their arm at the right elbow, and they need to try hard to resist you**.

Don't injure your athlete, coaches. For instance, if you're doing this to an 8yo, please offer enough tension to get them to bend. This isn't an arm wrestling match!

Now, **make sure the athlete notes how much force you used to bend their arm at the elbow while they're staring straight ahead**. Because this will be, what we compare to the following three-head-position variations…

One-Joint Rule Test, Step-1 with athlete's eyes straightforward.

You're now going to repeat the same process three more times, but you'll be changing the following head positions:

One-Joint Rule Test, Step-2 athlete has chin buried into chest.

1. Try bending their arm with their **chin buried into their chest**,
2. Try bending their arm **with their head back**, like they're looking into the sky, and
3. Try bending their arm **with their right ear as close to their right shoulder** as possible (for righty hitters, reverse for lefties).

Ask them which of the four-head-positions they felt the most stable and strength in resisting the bending arm.

If you did this right, then your athlete will find they were stronger and more stable at resisting you with their head staring straight ahead.

WHY?

What's going on here?

Dr. Kelly Starrett says this:

"The musculature [in the spine] *is designed to create stiffness so that you can effectively transmit energy to the primary engines of your hips and shoulders.* **If you don't preserve trunk stiffness while moving from your hips and shoulders, you will lose power and force.** *This is the basis for the one-joint rule: you should see flexion and extension movement happen at the hips and shoulders, not your spine."*

He then goes on to explain what I call 'kinking the performance hose':

"Hinging at one of the segments [vertebrae in the neck]*...when we put a hinge across the central nervous system, the body recognizes that as a primary insult, or threat to the body, because you're basically guillotining or kinking the nervous system.* **You've kinked 'the tube', so it** [force production] **just drops off."**

Extending and flexing the spine are fine, but it MUST be global, and not local.

Let's define those terms now...

One-Joint Rule Test, Step-3 athlete tips head back.

Global versus Local Flexion/Extension

Let's define what spinal flexion and extension are...

Spinal flexion would be like lying on your back and doing a crunch, sit-up, or standing and bending sideways at the hip. Other examples of this would be the Hollow Position in Gymnastics or the Child's Pose in Yoga.

Please search the latter two poses on Google Images or YouTube.

One-Joint Rule Test, Step-4 athlete moves same side ear and shoulder together.

Spinal extension would be like lying on your stomach and arching your chest and face away

from the ground, also known as a Back Extension in the gym. In Yoga, Upward- Facing-Dog Pose would be a good example of spinal extension.

Again, you can do a quick Google Images or YouTube search to get a clear picture of these.

For most, the lower-back, or Lumbar is always in a state of slight extension, also known as lordosis when the spine is in neutral.

Now,

Global Flexion or Extension of the spine is when the head and spine bend together, or the head follows the bending line of the spine.

Contrarily,

Local Flexion or Extension of the spine is when the one isolated section of the spine bends without the others.

This can be a solo bending of the neck OR lower-back.

An example of this would be any of the last three head positions described in the One-Joint Rule test I took you through above.

So, how does this apply to the swing?

Can Elite Hitters have Swing Flaws?

Have you heard these head/vision coaching cues…?

- "Get your nose behind the ball",
- "Keep your head down at contact",
- "Watch the ball as long as possible", Or
- **"Get eyes on plane of the pitch"**…

These are not good coaching cues for force production, or to the vertebrae in the neck. And besides, it's humanly impossible for a hitter to track the ball all the way to the bat. That's a talk for another day.

Did you know…?

Derek Jeter, Bryce Harper, and Prince Fielder move their rear ear into their rear shoulder at impact?

Unfortunately, **this may have had a devastating effect on Prince Fielder's career, causing him to retire early after a season ending spinal surgery that fused vertebra in his neck**. Similar to what Peyton Manning had done because of a football injury.

Fortunately for Derek Jeter, his spine wasn't affected like Fielder's.

And time will tell with Bryce Harper.

The same goes for Andrew McCutchen and Nolan Arenado, who bury their chin into the chest at impact. At some point, this too will take a toll.

I've had local and online hitters with these issues, in addition to one more…

…Where the head goes back at impact, like looking into the sky. I've never seen this head movement in Big League hitters, but that doesn't mean someone somewhere isn't doing this to some degree.

Whether I see my hitter's head doing any of the above, I make it a priority to fix right away.

As you can see from the One-Joint Rule Test I took you through above, when the neck is in a locally flexed (chin to chest, or rear ear into rear shoulder) or extended (head back) positions, then force is leaked.

Think about it this way…

A similar 'force leak' phenomenon happens when you have a blown sprinkler…the spray pressure of other sprinklers on the same line are dramatically affected.

The other, more important reason for making this head position a priority to fix is SAFETY. Watching McCutchen, Arenado, and Harper swing is painful for me to watch.

What I tend to see with my hitters after fixing this, is a dramatic jump in Ball Exit Speeds, AND their radar readings become more stable and less erratic.

The other good news is…

It's an easy fix.

The Neck Brace Hitting Drill

BIG thanks to Head Softball Coach, Todd Bradley at Campbell University for the Neck Brace Hitting Drill.

It's as simple as it sounds.

Get a foam neck brace on Amazon.com, either in a youth or adult size, depending on the size of the hitter or hitters.

It's not important to get one with a metal shunt in it because we're not trying to completely immobilize the head.

The objective of the drill is to give the hitter instant feedback for whenever their head wants to go back, sideways, or down. The head MUST be free to turn side to side, like motioning 'NO' with the head.

When a hitter has this swing flaw, use the neck brace generously, and then move them to wearing it sparingly. Obviously, we're moving the hitter to not have to wear it, and acting 'as if' the neck brace is still on.

When wearing it sparingly, I'd have the hitter wear it every other round of five cuts.

In between rounds, evaluate how they're maintaining the integrity of their spine, especially on the non-neck brace round.

Once they get pretty good with learning the proper motor-skill, I'd have them wear the neck brace after two to three rounds of five cuts without wearing it.

How long does this take to fix?

It depends on how long the hitter has had this flaw.

However, **if the hitter spends 4-5 days per week and at least 5-15 minutes each day in deep and deliberate practice using the Neck Brace Drill, then we could see mastery within 4-6 weeks.**

Here's a link to a blog post going into the Neck Brace Hitting Drill:

http://gohpl.com/neckbracedrill

You made it!

We're all done with the specific principles of *The Catapult Loading System*, and now I want to include the teaching logistics of how to make this stuff stick.

We'll be applying psychological principles to what author, Peter C. Brown calls, **the science of successful learning**, in his book, *Make It Stick*.

These learning "rules" are as important, if not more critical, than the effective mechanics themselves…

12

CHAPTER 12

*"A martial artist who drills exclusively to a set pattern of combat is losing his freedom. He is actually becoming a slave to a choice pattern and feels that the pattern is the real thing. It leads to stagnation because **the way of combat is never based on personal choice and fancies, but constantly changes from moment to moment, and the disappointed combatant will soon find out that his 'choice routine' lacks pliability."***
– *Bruce Lee*

The Science of Successful Learning

Before getting into the meat of this Chapter,

I assume, since you made it this far in the book, you're looking to dive deeper into the subject of 'Sticky Coaching'...

So, I've included three books you can pick up on Amazon.com *(if you haven't already)*:

- ***Make It Stick:*** *The Science of Successful Learning,* by Peter C. Brown
- ***The Talent Code:*** *Greatness isn't Born. It's Grown. Here's How,* by Daniel Coyle
- ***The Sports Gene:*** *Inside the Science of Extraordinary Athletes,* by David Epstein

In the following pages, I'm going to distill and apply the information contained in these books to teaching hitters.

Here's what we're going to cover in this CHAPTER:

- **How to train "game-ready" hitters**
- How to find out a player's dominant learning style in 5-mins
- How to apply 'training-ugly' principles to practice
- Coaching feedback and practice time: **how much is too much, and when is it not enough?**

Let's get started...

How to Train "Game Ready" Hitters

Why do you think one of the most asked questions I get is, how to transition grooved batting practice swings into game-swing performance?

To answer this common coaching challenge, let me tell you a story…

There was a young Greek boy, named Milo of Croton, who was told by his parents to carry their baby bull into town, to get milk and feed him.

Milo carried this bull into town day after day, week after week, and month after month.

The bull kept getting bigger with each passing day, and as a result, Milo also grew bigger and stronger.

This young Milo ended up becoming one of the most revered wrestlers in Greek history.

According to Sports-Training-Advisor.com,

"The Principle of Specificity refers to the type of changes the body makes in response to sports training. Very simply, what you do is what you get."

Milo got bigger and stronger because the bull's weight progressively increased.

So, what does the Principle of Specificity have to do with transitioning a five-o-clock hitter into a game crusher?

EVERYTHING!

In baseball or softball, imagine a "shot clock" between pitches.

What do you estimate that shot clock would count to?

10-20 seconds between pitches?

In addition, a hitter will get, on average, three chances to swing the bat…three strikes. Sometimes more or sometimes less…but let's use THREE as an average.

This same hitter may get FOUR at-bats per game.

So, this hitter may get TWELVE opportunities to swing the bat in a game.

Also, most likely, there will be more than 10-20 seconds between swings.

The point is this; **hitters MUST make every swing count.**

In addition, and unlike golf, there are two major elements included in competing at the plate…pitch selection, and being on-time.

If we're looking at the principle of Specificity – or *what you do is what you get* – then **what would training look like to address the environment of game swings?**

I'll give you an example of something that DOES NOT help hitters adapt to the demands of a game at-bat…

Would a drill like rapid fire soft toss or rapid fire batting practice help hitters? Tossing or throwing a batting practice pitch every 2-4 seconds…

NO.

Before you get into the argument, *"Well, that drill is for developing quick hands"*.

If that's what you're thinking, then you're missing the forest for the trees.

The hands get quicker and more forceful when the swing is driven by the Spinal Engine. In other words, quick hands without effective Spinal Engine mechanics, is like swatting flies.

Think about the force of a boxer's jab versus his knockout punch.

If the pitcher had three baseballs to start, and the name of the game was how efficient she could release those three pitches in quick succession to the hitter, then rapid fire soft and LIVE toss would be the way to train.

But it's not.

So how do we train hitters in the cages to maximize every swing?

1. **Make sure the hitter understands they should be breathing heavier after 5 swings.**
2. Only have hitters take three to five swings per round, and then take a short coach's evaluation break (more on giving feedback to hitters shortly).
3. As coach, take your time replacing the ball on a tee, or serving up another soft or LIVE toss…give the hitter a chance to reset.

Look, hitting is a sprint, not a marathon. More effort, higher intensity, less reps. In other words, you wouldn't do marathon training for a 100-meter sprint competition.

Hitting is not about taking 100 swings to get into a "groove" or "rhythm".

What do you think the swing intensity of a 50-pitch round batting practice looks like?

About 70% or less because the hitter would need to conserve energy to get through the long arse round!

What do you think practicing 70% swing intensity does to game timing, if in the game, the hitter is expected to use 100% swing intensity?

The hitter would have to start their swing much earlier in game at-bats to compensate for the variance in practice swings.

So why not practice 100% swing intensity in practice, so the hitter doesn't have to re-calibrate their timing in games?

The only time it's okay to turn down swing RPM's during practice is when working on something mechanically.

Before getting into "training ugly", I want to go over…

How to find out a Player's Dominant Learning Style in 5-mins

I mentioned a coach's evaluation between five-swing rounds…

It's during this time, coach will quiz the hitter to see how body aware they were with the swings they took.

It is in these questions, that you can learn a player's learning-style within minutes.

The VAK Model, as it is called, is according to the science of Neuro-Linguistic Programming, or NLP for short, which is what world-renown, public-speaker, Tony Robbins uses in his programs.

VAK stands for Visual, Auditory, and Kinesthetic (or feel).

A player's dominant learning style can be tipped off within minutes, by looking at where the hitter's eyes go immediately after being asked a question…

- **If the eyes go UP** and to the left or right, then they may be primarily a visual learner.
- **If the eyes go SIDE-TO-SIDE**, then they may be primarily an auditory learner. And,
- **If the eyes go DOWN** and to the left, right, or straight forward, then they may be primarily a kinesthetic (or feel) learner.

I say "may be primarily", because in 5 minutes, you're getting a ballpark estimate. Over time, with a particular hitter, you'll be more certain of their primary learning style.

You'll also notice their second "go-to" eye location, which is helpful if your primary learning style coaching cue doesn't seem to be working.

For instance, **if I notice a player's eyes consistently going down when answering my questions, and occasionally they go up…then I know that hitter has a primarily *feel* learning style with *visual* as secondary. So, I can play with those two.**

What are some coaching questions using the VAK model?

Visual cues:

- "Can you *see* what you just did there?"
- *"Look* at what you did on swing number-3…"
- "Was the difference between those swings *black and white*, or kind of *grey?*"

Auditory cues:

- "How did the *sound* of impact differ from swing one and swing four?"
- "Does the answer springy fascia *ring a bell?*"
- "Notice the *discord* at impact when you're off the sweet spot?"

Kinesthetic cues:

- "Can you *feel* the difference between the two swings?"
- "I want you to *hold* your swing position at landing…"
- "You hit that ball like a *ton of bricks!*"

Now, that you have this tool in your belt; let's move on to discussing…

How to Apply 'Training Ugly' Principles to Practice

I'm going to share with you a couple studies from Peter C. Brown's book, *Make It Stick*, to help illustrate this section…

Hitters of the Cal Poly baseball team were split up into two groups throughout the season.

Group one hitters are thrown the following pitches at practice:

- 15 fastballs,
- 15 curveballs, and
- 15 changeups.

Group two hitters are thrown a random mix of these three pitches at practice.

Which group do you think did better throughout the season?

The Massed Practice group one, also known as Blocked, Or the Random Practice group two?

Group one did better in the initial practice rounds, however group TWO did better throughout the season.

WHY?

A classroom of 4th graders were split up into two groups, A and B.

Group A practiced throwing bean bags into a bucket that was 3-feet away for 15 minutes.

Group B practiced throwing bean bags into two buckets, one was 2-feet away and the other was 4-feet away.

At the end of 15-minutes, both groups were tested throwing the bean bags in one 3-foot bucket…

Which group did better?

Group B did, who practiced throwing into the two buckets.

WHY?

Massed (or Blocked) Practice versus Random Practice

Why did the Cal Poly baseball study turn out like it did?

…and what about the bean bag study?

YouTuber Trevor Ragan gives this a name, 'Training Ugly'.

I like 'training goofy' because that's what if feels like, or using variance.

He says effectively learning a sport skill, requires three steps:

1. **Read**
2. **Plan**
3. **Do**

In the random-pitched group of Cal Poly baseball players, and the two-bucket distance bean bag group, the participants had to Read, Plan, and Do. The latter "Do" step is the execution of technique.

In the Massed or Block Practice groups, the "Read" and "Plan" steps were virtually removed from the motor-skill-acquisition-equation.

According to Random versus Block Practice studies in basketball, golf, and baseball, **this matters A LOT when transitioning and retaining sport skills into games because that's how the competitive environment is...seemingly random**.

And in those studies, skill retention rates went up in games over 40% more when Random Practice was instituted over Blocked.

For a young athlete, 'training ugly' or "goofy":

- Is more challenging,
- Will be more frustrating, and as a result, they'll make more mistakes,
- **Is better for them**, and
- Prepares them better for game situations.

We'll look at how to apply the 'Training Ugly' Principle to hitters in a moment, but first…

The Goldilocks Golden Rule

You've heard the story of *Goldilocks and the Three Bears*, right?

In the bears' kitchen, Goldilocks didn't want the porridge that was too hot or too cold, she wanted the one that was just right.

I talk to my hitters about mechanics this way.

Let me give you another example.

On the Hardcore History podcast, the host **shared how the Germans calibrated their big artillery fire at the trenches of the French and British during World War 1**.

The Allied Nations would be sitting in their 8-foot trench and hear a whistling overhead…and they'd watch a gigantic German artillery shell fly over their trenches, land and explode about one mile away.

Then, another whistling, but this time the gigantic German artillery shell would land about one mile in front of their open trench.

Guess where the next one landed…

Near their trench!! And from there on out, the British and French military forces were bombarded with reigning SUPER-heavy German artillery from overhead.

What were the Germans doing?

It has a name, according to Marine Colonel, Mark Coast, who's father to two of my hitters in San Diego, and who's a Primary Firearms and Tactical Instructor for Navy Seal and Marine snipers.

The Germans were doing what's called the 'Standard Artillery Round Adjustment Method'.

Again, coming back to the bean bag study and the Goldilocks Golden Rule.

So,

How to Apply 'Training Ugly' Principles to Practice?

The following, is what I use with my hitters on a daily basis, but is definitely not exhaustive of what you could come up with.

In other words, your imagination is your friend.

Here are some 'training ugly' ideas to get your creative juices flowing:

- **Moving tee after every swing** – up or down, inside or outside. I rarely put the tee right down the middle for my hitters. Just like in the Bean Bag Study…if they can hit the inside and outside pitch, then they'll hit it down the middle.
- **Varied-Reaction-LIVE-Toss-Timing-Drill (VRLTTD)** – my favorite drill for timing. I use two plates set about five to ten feet apart, and throw from a stationary L-screen. I then progress the hitter through the following depending on challenge level…Easy – hitter shifts plates after every 5-swing round…Medium – hitter shifts plates after every two swings, for a 6-swing round…Hard – hitter shifts plates after every two pitches, for a 5-swing round.
- **Reverse Strike-zone** – I just started doing this with my hitters. Hitter takes a five-swing round, hitting "strikes". Goes through a coach's evaluation, then does a five-swing round, hitting "balls". How does this benefit? This gives a hitter a better sense of the strike versus hitting zone, plus it fries their brain! Also, if you're pairing this with the VRLTTD drill above, make sure to start on the Easy progression.
- **Random-Pitch-Round** – think of the Cal Poly hitters in the random group from the study we looked at earlier. In a five-swing round, I'll mix 4-seam fastballs with either the circle change-up or a knuckleball…to minimize grip change in the glove. OR, I'll mix the 2-seam fastball and the curveball or cutter. The hitter works on hunting one of the two pitches in one round. Also with this, start on the Easy progression to VRLTTD.
- **Working mechanics** – in a 5-swing round, I'll have the hitter work the effective mechanics and its ineffective counterpart. For instance, if we're working on 'showing the numbers', then on the odd swings (1, 3, and 5), the hitter will 'show numbers'. And on the even swings, the hitter WILL NOT 'show numbers'. When doing this, please explain to your hitters you want them focusing on process, not results. In other words, if they 'show numbers' when they're supposed to, but swing and miss, they get an 'A' for that swing. If they don't 'show numbers' when they're supposed to, but hit a fiery hole through the back of the cage, then they get an 'F' for that swing.
- **Barrel awareness** – wind frog-tape around the sweet spot of the barrel, but with about a half inch gap between the tape. Tell your hitter to practice hitting the outside, middle, OR inside tape on all swings or for certain swings. Great drill for increasing batting average.
- **Barrel control** – hit on an open field and put markers out in the outfield, like you'd see at a golf course driving range. Have the hitter practice hitting the different markers in a particular order. They can stride however they like, to accomplish the swing objective. Another great drill for increasing batting average.
- **Hand-speed control** – have the hitter swing using different hand speeds, but still get positive launch angle. The coach throws the ball at different speeds, and the hitter matches. Great for adjusting to off speed.

You can thank Coach Lee Comeaux for the last three, coming from his golfing background, accuracy is EXTREMELY important. His 13-year-old daughter, who plays softball in Texas, hit over .600 in her league this past year with his teachings.

Giving Feedback to Hitters

Think back to when you were transitioning your kids from the bike with training wheels to a bike without…

Did you throw the training wheels away totally, or leave one on, allowing for the young one to lean on the training wheel side for safety?

Here's a clue…

The best way to get kids riding a bike without training wheels is…

Drum roll please…

…to have them ride the bike WITHOUT training wheels!!

Just kidding, I know you knew that. I was just giving you a metaphor for giving feedback to hitters. **Think of the training wheels as the frequency of feedback you give to your hitter or hitters.**

If you're constantly reminding them what they need to fix or are doing great at after each swing, then you're the bike with the training wheels still on.

Don't get me wrong,

I'm not saying zero feedback is the best way.

I want to remind you of the Goldilocks Golden Rule we covered a short while ago.

Highly frequent feedback or none at all are not effective; we want what's just right.

What's the happy medium for giving feedback to hitters?

Using our 5-swing rounds as an example…

I do my best to put my poker face on until the end of five swings. Occasionally I'll say, "okay", "alright", or "next" just to let them know to move to the next swing, but **I try to cloak my elation or disgust because I want them to ride the bike without me being the training wheels.**

Young athletes are FULLY capable of making adjustments on their own

I tell my hitters to listen to the little voices in their head…lol

No really…when there's high frequency feedback being given to them by outside sources (YOU!!), then that little problem-solving voice shuts up.

Here's a great example…

In his book, *Golf Flow*, Professor Gio Valiante, a Sports Performance Psychologist who works with top PGA tour golfers, recalls a class session where he teaches at Rollins College in Winter Park, Florida…

In the middle of a class session that was being video-recorded, he asked a female student to walk up and try her hand at sinking a putt on a 6-foot artificial green he had set up.

The first try was rushed, and she missed horribly beyond the cup.

The second try she took more time to line up and her putt came up a bit short.

The third try she took a little more time, made a few mechanical adjustments, then sank the putt!

Please note that during the test, not a word was said to her.

Dr. Gio Valiante then had everyone in the class watch the video back, and analyze what key adjustments she made after her misses.

The key here is that the female student made the adjustments on her own.

I tell my parents, your son or daughter figured out how to walk on their own. You didn't need to coach them. Gravity did. They figured out what stance is more stable, and which step to not make…on their own.

In-between swing rounds, I ask more questions than I give answers. It's like weekly quizzes in school. **Studies show, the more the brain has to work to remember something new, the stickier the lesson.**

The 3 Question Hitting Outcome Checklist

After a LIVE batting practice 5-swing round, I ask the following three questions:

1. **How many strikes did you swing at?**
2. **How many swings were on-time?** And,
3. **How did you do with [fill in the blank] hitting mechanic?**

And yes, in that order.

If they're not swinging at strikes (assuming they're not doing the reverse strike zone drill), then effective mechanics will break down.

If they're not on-time, then effective mechanics will be rendered ineffective.

The common conclusion players and coaches jump to is that a bad hitting outcome in the game is a result of bad mechanics.

Mechanics SHOULD BE the last thing to tinker with.

An example of a checklist question I'd ask in number three above would be,

Let's say the hitter is working on Finger Pressure in that round, specifically top hand, bottom-three-finger-pressure on all swings…

Then I'd ask them,

"What were the top two swings where you turned Finger Pressure on and off when you were supposed to?"

After they answered, then I'd follow up with,

"What was the worst swing, where you didn't turn Finger Pressure on or off when you were supposed to?"

It's important to note, that **this question MUST be skipped during and after game at-bats. Postgame is fine, but not during the game. Coaches, only focus on questions one and two during games.**

If it's not front of mind, then it will be forgotten.

That's the magic in asking these three questions between swing rounds. Some hitters will be more aware of these points than others, but others will need to dust off this part of the brain.

It's rare that I have a hitter that doesn't improve their plate discipline and timing after three 5-swing rounds of asking these questions. The more rounds taken, the better they get.

A coach's main teaching objective is to mold hitters who are self-correcting machines. Take those training-wheels off and let them fly!

How often should young hitters practice and how many swings per session?

I get asked this question quite a bit…

In my experience, **what I've found over the years is 4 to 5 days per week is the sweet spot for practice frequency.**

I ask my local hitters how many hitting homework days they got in during the week prior to this lesson, and if they respond with 1 to 3 days…

With almost 85% certainty. I know we'll have to review what we worked on the week before. With this practice frequency, some hitters may progress in the lessons; and others will be repeating a past lesson.

Looking at the slow-motion video, it's rare to get a hitter that spends less than 3 days with their hitting homework, and 100% progress forward on the next lesson.

How many swings per session is very important.

You've already read about the *Principle of Specificity* and the *Goldilocks Golden Rule*, so you should already have a clue that a hitter can take too many swings.

And obviously, not taking any swings isn't effective either, evidenced in the frequency of practice time we just talked about.

I've moved away from prescribing swings in quantity, to having my hitters work within an allotted time.

I tell my hitters to give me 5-minutes per day, for 4 to 5 days per week. I tell them to be happy if they get their 5-mins in…have mom or dad set a timer, and once it goes off, then they're done and can move on to video games.

Why only five minutes?

I want to set those less motivated or inspired hitters up for success, coaches you know who those are.

I already know the more motivated and inspired will put more time in and that's fine. But the objective is quality OVER quantity swings. Remember, **make every swing count.**

And their practice at home should somewhat resemble our 'training ugly' principles discussed earlier. Deliberate, deep practice as Daniel Coyle says in his book, *The Talent Code*.

The following section is written a little more formal than most of this book, and it's because I wrote this about 2-3 years ago, with the intent to publish a sticky coaching book, but I didn't feel it was complete.

I put a TON of research and study into the following information, so I know you'll love it…

Praise for effort, NOT for Talent

In this section, we'll be looking at:

- The "Praise-for" scientific study,
- Con's for Praise-for-intellect, and
- Five Reasons to Stop Saying "Good Job!"

This section is the heart and soul of *The Science of Sticky Coaching* book I published in February of 2017.

It can take loads of cerebral energy to change the syntax of what you're saying and how you're saying it. **The basic premise is to stop celebrating generalized outcomes – or results – and promote the work that got the result.**

In John Medina's book, *Brain Rules for Baby*, he says:

*"What separates high performers from low performers is not some divine spark. It is, the most recent findings suggest, a much more boring — but ultimately more controllable — factor. All other things being equal, it is EFFORT. **The ability to focus one's attention, and then sustain that focus. Effort also involves impulse control and a persistent ability to delay gratification.**"*

The "Praise-for" scientific study

In, *The Talent Code* by Daniel Coyle, he talked about Dr. Carol Dweck, a social psychologist at Stanford who's been studying motivation for thirty years.

She says,

*"Left to our own devices, we go along in a pretty stable mindset. But, **when we get a clear cue, a message that sends a spark, then boing, we respond.**"*

The following experiment tested what changing the arrangement of six words could do to a child's psychological performance…

Dr. Dweck did an experiment with 400 New York fifth-graders. Kids were given a test of fairly-easy puzzles, and afterwards were given a different mix of six-words.

She praised Group A with intelligence, *"You must be smart at this!"*

And she praised Group B for effort, *"You must have worked really hard."*

The Kids were tested a second time and were given the choice of a hard or easy test. Group A (praise-for-intellect) chose the easy test, while Group B (praise-for-effort) chose the hard test. Dweck explained,

"When we praise children for their intelligence, we tell them that's the name of the game: look smart, don't risk making mistakes."

The findings?

Quoted from, *The Talent Code*,

"The praise-for-effort group improved their initial score by 30%, while the praised-for-intelligence group's score declined by 20%. All because of six short words."

Daniel Coyle said that true to the Dweck study, in each of the athletic hotbeds he visited from around the world, **affirmed the value of effort and slow progress rather than innate talent or intelligence.**

Praise needs to be earned. In which case, we're affirming the struggle. Dweck notes that,

"Motivation does not increase with increased levels of praise but often dips."

Motivational language often used, refers to hopes, dreams, and affirmations ("Good job!" or "You're the best!" or "You're so talented!"). These statements are generalized, and therefore meaningless to performance.

Con's for Praise-for-intellect

The following ideas came from John Medina's, *Brain Rules for Baby*…

What happens psychologically when you say "You're so smart!"?

"First, your child begins to perceive mistakes as failures. Because you told her that success was due to some static ability over which she had no control, she starts to think of failure (such as a bad grade) as a static thing, too — now perceived as a lack of ability. Successes are thought of as gifts rather than the governable product of effort.

*Second, perhaps as a reaction to the first, **she becomes more concerned with looking smart, rather than with actually learning something**.*

*Third, **she becomes less willing to confront the reasons behind any deficiencies, less willing to make an effort. Such kids have a difficult time admitting errors. There is simply too much at stake for the future.***

What should you say?

'I'm so proud of you. You must have really studied hard.' This appeals to the controllable effort rather than to unchangeable talent. It's called 'growth mindset' praise."

Here's an article a good friend of mine sent me – who has a Master's Degree in Child Development. I've somewhat paraphrased it for you in following…

Five Reasons to Stop Saying "Good Job!"

Alfie Kohn authored and published this article in *Young Children's* magazine (2001). An abridged version of this article was published in *Parents* magazine in May 2000 with the title "Hooked on Praise." For a more detailed look at the issues discussed here — as well as a comprehensive list of citations to relevant research — please see the books *Punished by Rewards and Unconditional Parenting* by Alfie Kohn.

REASON #1: Manipulating Children

In the article, Rheta DeVries, a professor of education at the University of Northern Iowa, **talks about how saying "Good job!" can be referred to as "sugar-coated control."** This can look like tangible rewards – or even punishments because children are hungry for our approval.

It's a way of doing something for our children to comply with our wishes. As opposed to working with our children, such as asking them about how can what we've done affect other people…?

And in the words of Kohn:

"We have a responsibility not to exploit that dependence for our own convenience. A 'Good job!' to reinforce something that makes our lives a little easier can be an example of taking advantage of children's dependence. Kids may also come to feel manipulated by this, even if they can't quite explain why."

REASON #2: Creating Praise Junkies

We may praise kids with a 'Good job!' because we really want to bolster their self-esteem, but studies show the opposite actually happens. Praise like this can often make kids dependent on our feedback. Consider this study from the article:

"Mary Budd Rowe, a researcher at the University of Florida, discovered that students who were praised lavishly by their teachers were more tentative in their responses, more apt to answer in a questioning tone of voice ("Um, seven?"). They tended to back off from an idea they had proposed as soon as an adult disagreed with them. And they were less likely to persist with difficult tasks or share their ideas with other students."

In other words, **'Good Job' praise makes a child feel more insecure than secure with themselves.**

REASON #3: Stealing a Child's Pleasure

A child has the right to take pride in what they've learned how to do or done better than they did the last time. An adult telling them 'Good job!' is deciding – for the child – what to feel and when to feel it.

This is a form of positive judgment, just like 'Bad job!' would be a form of negative judgment. And just like adults, kids don't like to be judged.

In the words of Kohn:

*"I cherish the occasions when my daughter manages to do something for the first time, or does something better than she's ever done it before. But I try to resist the knee-jerk tendency to say, "Good job!" because I don't want to dilute her joy. **I want her to share her pleasure with me, not look to me for a verdict. I want her to exclaim, 'I did it!' (which she often does) instead of asking me uncertainly, 'Was that good?'"***

REASON #4: Losing Interest

"Good job!" may get children to keep doing what they did to get the praise, but early childhood education expert Lilian Katz warns, "Once attention is withdrawn, many kids won't touch the activity again." Now, **the point isn't to draw, to read, to think, to create – the point is to get the goody, whether it's an ice cream, a sticker, or a "Good job!"**

In a study by Joan Grusec at the University of Toronto, young children who were frequently praised for displays of generosity tended to be slightly *less* generous on an everyday basis than other children were. Generosity became a means to an end.

Does praise motivate kids? Sure. It motivates kids to get praise.

REASON #5: Reducing Achievement

As Kohn says:

"Researchers keep finding that kids who are praised for doing well at a creative task tend to stumble at the next task – and they don't do as well as children who weren't praised to begin with.

Why does this happen? Partly, because the praise creates pressure to 'keep up the good work' that gets in the way of doing so. Partly, because their interest in what they're doing may have declined. Partly, because they become less likely to take risks – a prerequisite for creativity – once they start thinking about how to keep those positive comments coming."

World-renown public speaker, Anthony Robbins, always talks about the power of word-syntax. Changing words around can make a big difference. For instance, *"The dog bit Johnny,"* versus *"Johnny bit the dog."* Same words, but gives the sentence a dramatically different meaning, as Robbins says, *"especially for Johnny!".*

Changing the way you praise young athletes can make them work harder for you. AND, they also get the benefit of not feeling manipulated, getting their independence, pleasure, interest, and sense of achievement taken away.

Examples for coaches to change syntax

My friend Kari Applegate, with the Master's Degree in Child Development, shared a PDF with me that **she developed for her parents on changing word-syntax to more productively communicate (praise-for-effort) with their children.**

The following PDF goes into different situations and details, so I highly suggest you CLICK the following link, or input it in your favorite browser, print it out, and study it…

http://gohpl.com/praise4effortpdf

In this section, we looked at:

- The "Praise-for" scientific study,
- Con's for Praise-for-intellect, and
- Five Reasons to Stop Saying "Good Job!"

CONCLUSION

Well, you made it to the end of the book.

This puts you in a highly-specialized category of readers.

I heard a statistic somewhere that **10% of people who buy books actually finish them!**

Making it this far shows you're an action taker, and most likely have a Growth Mindset.

First, I want to review what you just learned in this STEP-BY-STEP guide for coaches...

- Discovered a principles-based hitting approach versus the uncertainty of a hitting philosophy or theory,
- Learned WHY video analysis comes second to understanding human-movement-principles validated by science,
- **How YOU can be a hitting expert, even if your playing experience is Little League**,
- Found out how to put together powerfully revealing swing-experiments,
- Learned from Thomas Myers's the science of springy fascia, and from Dr. Serge Gracovetsky's The Spinal Engine,
- Read about the certainty of power and fixing bad habits by using Finger Pressure, the Hunched Posture, Showing Numbers, Downhill Shoulders, Hiding the Hands, and the One-Joint Rule,
- And lastly, you learned **how to effectively transition grooved-batting-practice-swings into game at-bats**, the magic of 'training ugly', giving hitters feedback, and how to praise for effort.

WHAT did I want you to get out of this book?

My goal is to equip hitting coaches with physical and psychological tools that work on a consistent basis – and that are validated by science, **so you can help positively affect more hitters around the world**.

WHY do I want to get this information into your hands?

Well, according to the Little League Baseball and Softball participation statistics following the 2008 season, there were nearly 2.6 million players in Little League Baseball worldwide, including both boys and girls, including 400,000 registered in softball (also including both boys and girls).

That was over 8 years ago!

I've heard the numbers are now between EIGHT and SIXTEEN million worldwide now.

The problem is retention.

We're bringing in record numbers, but not retaining them.

There are a host of reasons why this is case, and would probably fill up a whole other book, but I think one of the biggest issues is misinformation on HOW TO succeed at our sport.

Here are my FOUR leading causes of misinformation out there:

- **YouTube & Google** – what I find is great people with knowledge are poor marketers, and people with poor knowledge are great marketers. Great information gets buried on the net!

- **Social Media Bullying** – the vocal Trolls. Not treasure Trolls, but the knuckleheads that know enough to be dangerous. I have a bank of screenshot comments on my computer to prove it.
- **Explosion of Travel Ball** – more teams means dilution of the talent pool, paid coaches who shouldn't be getting paid, all about reps not substance, more Fixed Mindset coaches versus Growth Mindset coaches, all about winning early on and not development, and on and on.
- **Unknowledgeable Market Influencers** – just because 'staying short to the ball' or 'swinging down on the ball' works for elite athletes, doesn't mean it works for a majority of young hitters. There's a difference between what's *real* and what's *feel*. MLB and pro-players in the coaching world are highly influential, for good reason. But coaching is a totally different world, and much of the *real* v. *feel* coaching cues get lost in translation.

You could probably think of a dozen more, but the point is **the right information isn't get into the right hands**.

And I want to contribute information to the hitting world that consistently works. Not only is the information contained in this book validated by human-movement-science,

- It shows up in elite hitters and other high-level explosive-rotational-athletes,
- **Inferior mechanics get "weeded out" in swing experiments**,
- Has been shown to work "in the trenches", AND most importantly,
- Hundreds of other coaches across the nation are using the same information and getting the similar results – if not better – than I am with my own hitters!

There is quite a hitting movement that's been brewing over the past few years. And it's not too late to jump on board today.

Help us empower hitters around the nation to consistently triple their body-weight in batted ball distance. Jump in and share your own hitting experiments. This is how the battle WILL be won coaches! It doesn't have to be a pissing contest anymore that's based on flimsy hitting philosophy and theory.

If you want to find the Hitting Performance Lab online, then you can at the following places:

- **"Like" us on Facebook** – over 23K+ Likes: https://www.facebook.com/HittingPerformanceLab/ (*you can also search "Hitting Performance Lab" on Facebook and we'll come up*)
- **Follow us on Twitter** – 4,300+ Followers: @hitperformlab (or visit: https://twitter.com/hitperformlab)
- **Subscribe to our YouTube channel** – 4,300+ organic Subscribers: https://www.youtube.com/user/HittingPerformLab (*you can also search "Hitting Performance Lab" on YouTube and we'll come up*)
- **Connect with Joey on Linkedin** – 700+ connections: https://www.linkedin.com/in/joeymyers30

If you're interested in some of our online video courses (*over 2,000 SOLD*), then you can learn more at the following link:

http://gohpl.com/hplcourses

If you're interested in the **online lesson training program** *The Feedback Lab*, then you can learn more at the following link:

http://gohpl.com/feedbacklab

For purchasing this book, I want to make you a deal to get access to all my online video courses with the following...

To purchase FOREVER access to all courses and SAVE $91, then please go to the following link:

http://gohpl.com/webinaronlybundle

To take advantage of **low monthly access to ALL courses with a 14-Day $1 Trial**, then please go to the following link:

http://gohpl.com/14daydollartrial

Make sure that you're swinging smarter by moving better.

And coaches, remember to...

"Go forth and make awesomeness."

– Unknown

THE SCIENCE OF STICKY COACHING: HOW TO TURN ORDINARY ATHLETES INTO EXTRAORDINARY

Grab your copy of: *The Science Of Sticky Coaching: How To Turn Ordinary Athletes Into Extraordinary* book on sale at Amazon today, at the following link:

http://gohpl.com/soscbook

From the back cover:

Discover How-To Teach, What to Teach, and How Athletes Optimally Learn By Doing What the Top 1% of Coaches Do

This *The Science of Sticky Coaching: How to Turn Ordinary Athletes into Extraordinary* book is split up into three sections:

1. **KNOWLEDGE** – (How-To Teach, Doing Things Right, "Effectiveness"): equipping inexperienced coaches, parents, and organizational leaders on how to effectively run their associations and teams,

2. **LEARNING** – (How they learn) – the science of successful learning, optimizing how young athletes acquire new skills, and maintaining a rich soil for learning, and

3. **DEVELOPMENT** – (What to teach, Doing the Right Things, "Efficiency"): training crucial fundamentals like playing catch, opposite field hitting, and throwing strikes and locating pitches.

After surveying tens of thousands of my email subscribers, specific thorn-in-the-side frustrations for coaches coaching Little League and 12u softball kept coming up. So this book is an attempt to address all these frustrations using science and what the top 1% of coaches are doing to handle them.

Go to the following link to grab your copy on Amazon:

http://gohpl.com/soscbook

ABOUT THE AUTHOR

My Name is Joey Myers, and I'm the founder of the Hitting Performance Lab. I played four years of Division-1 baseball at Fresno State from 2000-2003.

I'm a member of the **American Baseball Coaches Association** (ABCA), the **International Youth and Conditioning Association** (IYCA), and the **Society for American Baseball Research**(SABR). I'm also partnered with the **Positive Coaching Alliance** (PCA).

I'm a certified Youth Fitness Specialist (YFS) through the International Youth Conditioning Association (IYCA), Corrective Exercise Specialist (CES) through the National Academy of Sports Medicine (NASM), and Vinyasa yoga instructor...AND, I'm also certified in the Functional Muscle Screen (FMS).

I've spent 11+ years in the corrective fitness field, and have a passionate curiosity to help other players – just like yours – dramatically improve performance through the science of human movement.

I'm currently living in Fresno, CA with my wife Tiffany Myers and two kids, Noah (4yo boy) and Gracen (9mo old girl).

Made in the USA
Middletown, DE
28 October 2017